On the *Revival of the Religious Sciences* (*Iḥyāʾ ʿulūm al-dīn*)

"The *Iḥyāʾ ʿulūm al-dīn* is the most valuable and most beautiful of books."

—Ibn Khallikān (d. 681/1282)

"The *Iḥyāʾ ʿulūm al-dīn* is one of al-Ghazālī's best works."

—Aḥmad b. ʿAbd al-Ḥalīm (d. 728/1328)

"Any seeker of [felicity of] the hereafter cannot do without the *Iḥyāʾ ʿulūm al-dīn*"

—Tāj al-Dīn al-Subkī (d. 771/1370)

"The *Iḥyāʾ ʿulūm al-dīn* is a marvelous book containing a wide variety of Islamic sciences intermixed with many subtle accounts of Sufism and matters of the heart."

—Ibn Kathīr (d. 774/1373)

"The *Iḥyāʾ ʿulūm al-dīn* is one of best and greatest books on admonition, it was said concerning it, 'if all the books of Islam were lost except for the *Iḥyāʾ* it would suffice what was lost.'"

—Ḥājjī Khalīfa Kātib Čelebī (d. 1067/1657)

"The *Iḥyāʾ* [*ʿulūm al-dīn*] is one of [Imām al-Ghazālī's] most noble works, his most famous work, and by far his greatest work'"

—Muḥammad Murtaḍā l-Zabīdī (d. 1205/1791)

On Imām al-Ghazālī

"Al-Ghazālī is [like] a deep ocean [of knowledge]."

—Imām al-Ḥaramayn al-Juwaynī (d. 478/1085)

"Al-Ghazālī is the second [Imām] Shāfiʿī."

—Muḥammad b. Yaḥyā l-Janzī (d. 549/1154)

"Abū Ḥāmid al-Ghazālī, the Proof of Islam (Ḥujjat al-Islām) and the Muslims, the Imām of the *imāms* of religion, [is a man] whose like eyes have not seen in eloquence and elucidation, and speech and thought, and acumen and natural ability."

—ʿAbd al-Ghāfir b. Ismāʿīl al-Fārisī (d. 529/1134)

"[He was] the Proof of Islam and Muslims, Imām of the imāms of religious sciences, one of vast knowledge, the wonder of the ages, the author of many works, and [a man] of extreme intelligence and the best of the sincere."

—Imām al-Dhahabī (d. 748/1347)

"Al-Ghazālī is without doubt the most remarkable figure in all Islam."

—T.J. DeBoer

". . . A man who stands on a level with Augustine and Luther in religious insight and intellectual vigor."

—H.A.R. Gibb

"I have to some extent found, and I believe others can find, in the words and example of al-Ghazālī a true *iḥyāʾ* . . ."

—Richard J. McCarthy, S.J.

وَأَذِّن فِي ٱلنَّاسِ
بِٱلۡحَجِّ يَأۡتُوكَ رِجَالٗا وَعَلَىٰ كُلِّ
ضَامِرٖ يَأۡتِينَ مِن كُلِّ فَجٍّ عَمِيقٖ ٢٧

And proclaim to the people the hajj [pilgrimage]; they will come to you on foot and on every lean camel; they will come from every distant pass.

Sūrat al-Ḥajj
22:27

The Forty Books of the Revival of the Religious Sciences (*Iḥyāʾ ʿulūm al-dīn*)

The Quarter of Worship

1 The Book of Knowledge
2 The Principles of the Creed
3 The Mysteries of Purification
4 The Mysteries of the Prayer
5 The Mysteries of Charity
6 The Mysteries of Fasting
7 **The Mysteries of the Pilgrimage**
8 The Etiquette of the Recitation of the Qurʾān
9 Invocations and Supplications
10 The Arrangement of the Litanies and the Exposition of the Night Vigil

The Quarter of Customs

11 The Proprieties of Eating
12 The Proprieties of Marriage
13 The Proprieties of Acquisition and Earning a Living
14 The Lawful and the Unlawful
15 The Proprieties of Friendship and Brotherhood
16 The Proprieties of Retreat
17 The Proprieties of Travel
18 The Proprieties of the Audition and Ecstasy
19 The Commanding of Right and the Forbidding of Wrong
20 The Proprieties of Living and the Prophetic Mannerisms

The Quarter of Perils

21 The Exposition of the Wonders of the Heart
22 Training the Soul, Refining the Character, and Treating the Ailments of the Heart
23 Overcoming the Two Desires
24 The Bane of the Tongue
25 The Censure of Anger, Malice, and Envy
26 The Censure of This World
27 The Censure of Greed and the Love of Wealth
28 The Censure of Fame and Hypocritical Ostentation
29 The Censure of Pride and Vanity
30 The Censure of Deceit

The Quarter of Deliverance

31 On Repentance
32 On Patience and Thankfulness
33 On Fear and Hope
34 On Poverty and Abstinence
35 On Unity and Trust
36 On Love, Longing, Intimacy, and Contentment
37 On Intention, Sincerity, and Truthfulness
38 On Vigilance and Accounting
39 On Contemplation
40 On the Remembrance of Death and the Hereafter

THE MYSTERIES OF THE PILGRIMAGE AND ITS IMPORTANT ELEMENTS

Kitāb asrār al-ḥajj wa-muhimmātihā

Book 7 of

Iḥyāʾ ʿulūm al-dīn

The Revival of the Religious Sciences

بِسْمِ ٱللَّهِ ٱلرَّحْمَٰنِ ٱلرَّحِيمِ

AL-GHAZĀLĪ

Kitāb asrār al-ḥajj

THE MYSTERIES OF THE PILGRIMAGE

Book 7 of the *Iḥyāʾ ʿulūm al-dīn*

THE REVIVAL OF THE RELIGIOUS SCIENCES

Translated *from the* Arabic
with an Introduction *and* Notes
by M. Abdurrahman Fitzgerald

Fons Vitae
2020

The Mysteries of the Pilgrimage and its Important Elements, Book 7 of *The Revival of the Religious Sciences* first published in 2020 by

Fons Vitae
49 Mockingbird Valley Drive
Louisville, KY 40207 USA

www.fonsvitae.com

The Fons Vitae Ghazali Series
Library of Congress Control Number: 2020941759
ISBN 978-1-94-1610-49-7

Copyediting and indexing: Valerie Joy Turner
Book design and typesetting: www.scholarlytype.com
Text typeface: Adobe Minion Pro 11/13.5

Cover art courtesy of National Library of Egypt, Cairo. Qurʾānic frontispiece to part 19. Written and illuminated by ʿAbdallāh b. Muḥammad al-Ḥamadānī for Sultan Uljaytu 713/1313. Hamadan.

Printed in Canada

Contents

Editor's Note

This is the complete translation of the *Kitāb asrār al-ḥajj*, *The Mysteries of the Pilgrimage*, book 7 of the *Iḥyāʾ ʿulūm al-dīn* of Ḥujjat al-Islām, Abū Ḥāmid al-Ghazālī. It was translated from the published Arabic text of volume 2, pp. 129–254 by Dār al-Minhāj of Jedda (2011), which utilized additional manuscripts and early printed editions.

Arabic terms that appear in italics follow the transliteration system of the *International Journal of Middle East Studies*. Common era (CE) dates have been added. The blessings on prophets and others, as used by Imām al-Ghazālī, are represented in the original Arabic, as listed below.

Arabic	English	Usage
عَزَّوَجَلَّ	Mighty and majestic is He	On mention of God
سُبْحَانَهُ وَتَعَالَىٰ	Exalted and most high is He	Used together or separately
صَلَّىٱللَّهُ عَلَيْهِ وَسَلَّمَ	Blessings and peace of God be upon him	On mention of the Prophet Muḥammad
عَلَيْهِ ٱلسَّلَامُ	Peace be upon him	On mention of one
عَلَيْهِمُ ٱلسَّلَامُ	Peace be upon them	or more prophets
رَضِيَ ٱللَّهُ عَنْهُ	God be pleased with him	On mention of one or more
رَضِيَ ٱللَّهُ عَنْهُمْ	God be pleased with them	Companions of the Prophet
رَضِيَ ٱللَّهُ عَنْهَا	God be pleased with her	On mention of a female Companion of the Prophet
رَحِمَهُ ٱللَّهُ	God have mercy on him	On mention of someone who is deceased

The translators have included some of the footnotes and references provided by the editors of the Dār al-Minhāj edition.

These footnotes include comments from Murtaḍā l-Zabīdī's *Itḥāf* (a detailed commentary on the *Iḥyāʾ ʿulūm al-dīn*) and identify many of Imām al-Ghazālī's sources. The translators and editors have provided explanatory footnotes where necessary; clarification in the text appears in hard brackets.

Note that the terminology used to refer to the areas related to the pilgrimage can be somewhat confusing in English. The house, or ancient house (*al-bayt al-aṭīq*) or sacred house, refers to the mosque complex surrounding the Kaʿba (often called *al-ḥaram* or *al-ḥaram al-Makkī*), but it sometimes also refers to the Kaʿba itself. The term sanctuary denotes both the mosque complex (the *ḥaram*) and the larger area beyond Mecca that includes the other pilgrimage sites (i.e., ʿArafa, Muzdalifa, Minā). In addition, the mosque complex indicates the uncovered/open-air area around the Kaʿba, as well as the covered areas beyond that. By way of clarification, where 'house' refers to the mosque complex, the editors have added [complex] and where it refers to the Kaʿba itself, [Kaʿba] has been added.

In addition, the editors have compiled a short biography of Imām al-Ghazālī with a chronology of important events in his life. This is followed by an extract from Imām al-Ghazālī's introduction to the *Iḥyāʾ ʿulūm al-dīn*; the editors hope this may serve as a guide to the *Revival of the Religious Sciences* for those reading Imām al-Ghazālī for the first time.

Biography of Imām al-Ghazālī

He is Abū Ḥāmid Muḥammad b. Muḥammad b. Muḥammad b. Aḥmad al-Ghazālī al-Ṭūsī; he was born in 450/1058 in the village of Ṭābarān near Ṭūs (in northeast Iran) and he died there, at the age of fifty-five, in 505/1111. Muḥammad's father died when he and his younger brother Aḥmad were still young; their father left a little money for their education in the care of a Sufi friend of limited means. When the money ran out, their caretaker suggested that they enroll in a *madrasa*. The *madrasa* system meant they had a stipend, room, and board. Al-Ghazālī studied *fiqh* in his hometown under a Sufi named Aḥmad al-Rādhakānī; he then traveled to Jurjān and studied under Ismāʿīl b. Masʿada al-Ismāʿīlī (d. 477/1084).

On his journey home his caravan was overtaken by highway robbers who took all of their possessions. Al-Ghazālī went to the leader of the bandits and demanded his notebooks. The leader asked, what are these notebooks? Al-Ghazālī answered: "This is the knowledge that I traveled far to acquire," the leader acquiesced to al-Ghazālī's demands after stating: "If you claim that it is knowledge that you have, how can we take it away from you?" This incident left a lasting impression on the young scholar. Thereafter, he returned to Ṭūs for three years, where he committed to memory all that he had learned thus far.

In 469/1077 he traveled to Nīshāpūr to study with the leading scholar of his time, Imām al-Ḥaramayn al-Juwaynī (d. 478/1085), at the Niẓāmiyya College; al-Ghazālī remained his student for approximately eight years, until al-Juwaynī died. Al-Ghazālī was one of his most illustrious students, and al-Juwaynī referred to him as "a deep ocean [of knowledge]." As one of al-Juwaynī star pupils, al-Ghazālī used to fill in as a substitute lecturer in his teacher's absence. He also tutored his fellow students in the subjects that al-Juwaynī taught at the Niẓāmiyya. Al-Ghazālī wrote his first book, on the founding principles of legal theory (*uṣūl al-fiqh*), while studying with al-Juwaynī.

Very little is known about al-Ghazālī's family, though some biographers mention that he married while in Nīshāpūr; others note that he had married in Ṭūs prior to leaving for Nīshāpūr. Some accounts state that he had five children, a son who died early and four daughters. Accounts also indicate that his mother lived to see her son rise to fame and fortune.

After the death of al-Juwaynī, al-Ghazālī went to the camp (*al-muʿaskar*) of the Saljūq *wazīr* Niẓām al-Mulk (d. 485/1192). He stayed at the camp, which was a gathering place for scholars, and quickly distinguished himself among their illustrious company. Niẓām al-Mulk recognized al-Ghazālī's genius and appointed him professor at the famed Niẓāmiyya College of Baghdad.

Al-Ghazālī left for Baghdad in 484/1091 and stayed there four years—it was a very exciting time to be in the heart of the Islamic empire. At the Niẓāmiyya College he had many students, by some estimates as many as three hundred. In terms of his scholarly output, this was also a prolific period in which he wrote *Maqāṣid al-falāsifa, Tahāfut al-falāsifa, al-Mustaẓhirī,* and other works.

Al-Ghazālī was well-connected politically and socially; we have evidence that he settled disputes related to the legitimacy of the rule of the ʿAbbāsid caliph, al-Mustaẓhir (r. 487–512/1094–1118) who assumed his role as the caliph when he was just fifteen years old, after the death of his father al-Muqtadī (d. 487/1094). Al-Ghazālī issued a *fatwā* of approval of the appointment of al-Mustaẓhir and was present at the oath-taking ceremony.

In Baghdad, al-Ghazālī underwent a spiritual crisis, during which he was overcome by fear of the punishment of the hellfire. He became convinced that he was destined for the hellfire if he did not change his ways; he feared that he had become too engrossed in worldly affairs, to the detriment of his spiritual being. He began to question his true intentions: was he writing and teaching to serve God, or because he enjoyed the fame and fortune that resulted from his lectures. He experienced much suffering, both inward and outward; one day as he stood before his students to present a lecture, he found himself unable to speak. The physicians were unable to diagnose any physical malady. Al-Ghazālī remained in Baghdad for a time, then left his teaching post for the pilgrimage. He left behind fortune, fame, and influence. He was beloved by his numerous students and had many admirers, including the sultan; he was also envied by many. The presumption is that he left in the manner he did—ostensibly to undertake the pilgrimage—because if he had made public his intentions to leave permanently, those around him would have tried to convince him to remain and the temptation might have been too strong to resist.

After leaving Baghdad, he changed direction and headed toward Damascus; according to his autobiography he disappeared from the intellectual scene for ten years. This does not mean that he did not teach, but that he did not want to return to public life and be paid for teaching. This ten-year period can be divided into two phases. First, he spent two years in the East—in greater Syria and on the pilgrimage. We have evidence that while on his return to Ṭūs he appeared at a Sufi lodge opposite the Niẓāmiyya College in Baghdad. He spent the second phase of the ten-year period (the remaining eight years) in Ṭūs, where he wrote the famed *Iḥyāʾ ʿulūm al-dīn*, a work that was inspired by the change in his outlook that resulted from his spiritual crisis.

When he arrived back in his hometown in 490/1097, he established a school and a Sufi lodge, in order to continue teaching and learning. In 499/1106, Niẓām al-Mulk's son, Fakhr al-Mulk, requested that al-Ghazālī accept a teaching position at his old school, the Niẓāmiyya of Nīshāpūr. He accepted and taught for a time, but left this position in 500/1106 after Fakhr al-Mulk was assassinated by Ismāʿīlīs. He then returned to Ṭūs and divided his time between teaching and worship. He died in 505/1111 and was buried in a cemetery near the citadel of Ṭābarān.

Legacy and Contributions of al-Ghazālī

Al-Ghazālī's two hundred and seventy-three works span many disciplines and can be grouped under the following headings:

1. Jurisprudence and legal theory. Al-Ghazālī made foundational contributions to Shāfiʿī jurisprudence; his book *al-Wajīz* is major handbook that has been used in teaching institutions around the world; many commentaries have been written on it, most notably by Abū l-Qāsim ʿAbd al-Karīm al-Rāfiʿī (d. 623/1226). In legal theory, *al-Mustaṣfa min ʿilm al-uṣūl* is considered one of five foundational texts in the discipline.
2. Logic and philosophy. Al-Ghazālī introduced logic in Islamic terms that jurists could understand and utilize. His works on philosophy include the *Tahāfut al-falāsifa*, which has been studied far beyond the Muslim world and has been the subject of numerous commentaries, discussions, and refutations.
3. Theology, including works on heresiography in refutation of Bāṭinī doctrines. He also expounded on the theory of occasionalism.
4. Ethics and educational theory. The *Mīzān al-ʿamal* and other works such as the *Iḥyāʾ ʿulūm al-dīn* mention a great deal on education.
5. Spirituality and Sufism. His magnum opus, the *Iḥyāʾ ʿulūm al-dīn* is a pioneering work in the field of spirituality, in terms of its organization and its comprehensive scope.
6. Various fields. Al-Ghazālī also wrote shorter works in a variety of disciplines, including his autobiography (*al-Munqidh min al-ḍalāl*), works on Qurʾānic studies (*Jawāhir al-Qurʾān*), and political statecraft (*Naṣiḥat al-mūluk*).

Chronology of al-Ghazālī's Life

450/1058	Birth of al-Ghazālī at Ṭūs
c. 461/1069	Began studies at Ṭūs
c. 465/1073	Traveled to Jurjān to study
466–469/1074–1077	Studied at Ṭūs
469/1077	Studied with al-Jūwaynī at the Niẓāmiyya college in Nīshāpūr
473/1080	al-Ghazālī composed his first book, *al-Mankhūl fi l-uṣūl*
477/1084	Death of al-Fāramdhī, one of al-Ghazālī's teachers
25 Rabīʿ II 478/ 20 August 1085	Death of al-Jūwaynī; al-Ghazālī left Nīshāpūr
Jumāda I 484/ July 1091	Appointed to teach at the Niẓāmiyya college in Baghdad
10 Ramaḍān 485/ 14 October 1092	Niẓām-al-Mulk was assassinated
484–487/1091–1094	Studied philosophy
Muḥarrām 487/ February 1094	Attended the oath-taking of the new caliph, al-Mustaẓhir
487/1094	Finished *Maqāṣid al-falāsifa*
5 Muḥarrām 488/ 21 January 1095	Finished *Tahāfut al-falāsifa*
Rajab 488/ July 1095	Experienced a spiritual crisis
Dhū l-Qaʿda 488/ November 1095	Left Baghdad for Damascus
Dhū l-Qaʿda 489/ November – December 1096	Made pilgrimage and worked on the *Iḥyāʾ ʿulūm al-dīn*
Jumāda II 490/ May 1097	Taught from the *Iḥyāʾ ʿulūm al-dīn* during a brief stop in Baghdad
Rajab 490/June 1097	Seen in Baghdad by Abū Bakr b. al-ʿArabī
Fall 490/1097	Returned to Ṭūs

Dhū l-Ḥijja 490/ November 1097	Established a *madrasa* and a *khānqāh* in Ṭūs
Dhū l-Qaʿda 499/ July 1106	Taught at the Niẓāmiyya college in Nīshāpūr
500/1106	Wrote *al-Munqidh min al-ḍalāl*
500/1106	Returned to Ṭūs
28 Dhū l-Ḥijja 502/ 5 August 1109	Finished *al-Mustaṣfā min ʿilm al-uṣūl*
Jumada I 505/ December 1111	Finished *Iljām al-ʿawām ʿan ʿilm al-kalām*
14 Jumada II 505/ 18 December 1111	Imām al-Ghazālī died in Ṭūs

Eulogies in Verse

Because of him the lame walked briskly,
And the songless through him burst into melody.

On the death of Imām al-Ghazālī, Abū l-Muẓaffar Muḥammad al-Abiwardī said of his loss:

He is gone! and the greatest loss which ever afflicted me,
was that of a man who left no one like him among mankind.

About the *Revival of the Religious Sciences*

THE present work is book 7 of Imām al-Ghazālī's forty-volume masterpiece. Below is an excerpt from al-Ghazālī's introduction that explains the arrangement and purpose of the *Iḥyāʾ ʿulūm al-dīn.*

People have composed books concerning some of these ideas, but this book [the *Iḥyāʾ*] differs from them in five ways, by

1. clarifying what they have obscured and elucidating what they have treated casually;
2. arranging what they scattered and putting in order what they separated;
3. abbreviating what they made lengthy and proving what they reported;
4. omitting what they have repeated; and
5. establishing the truth of certain obscure matters that are difficult to understand and which have not been presented in books at all.

For although all the scholars follow one course, there is no reason one should not proceed independently and bring to light something unknown, paying special attention to something his colleagues have forgotten. Or they are not heedless about calling attention to it, but they neglect to mention it in books. Or they do not overlook it, but something prevents them from exposing it [and making it clear].

So these are the special properties of this book, besides its inclusion of all these various kinds of knowledge.

Two things induced me to arrange this book in four parts. The first and fundamental motive is that this arrangement in establishing what is true and in making it understandable is, as it were, inevitable because the branch of knowledge by which one approaches the hereafter is divided into the knowledge of [proper] conduct and the knowledge of [spiritual] unveiling.

By the knowledge of [spiritual] unveiling I mean knowledge and only knowledge. By the science of [proper] conduct I mean knowledge as well as action in accordance with that knowledge. This work will deal only with the science of [proper] conduct, and not with [spiritual] unveiling, which one is not permitted to record in writing, although it is the ultimate aim of saints and the ultimate aim of the sincere. The science of [proper] conduct is merely a path that leads to unveiling and only through that path did the prophets of God communicate with the people and lead them to Him. Concerning [spiritual] unveiling, the prophets عَلَيْهِمُ السَّلَامُ spoke only figuratively and briefly through signs and symbols, because they realized the inability of people's minds to comprehend. Therefore since the scholars are heirs of the prophets, they cannot but follow in their footsteps and emulate their way.

The knowledge of [proper] conduct is divided into (1) outward knowledge, by which I mean knowledge of the senses and (2) inward knowledge, by which I mean knowledge of the functions of the heart.

The physical members either perform acts of prescribed worship, or acts that are in accordance with custom, while the heart, because it is removed from the senses and belongs to the world of dominion, is subject to either praiseworthy or blameworthy [influences]. Therefore it is necessary to divide this branch of knowledge into two parts: outward and inward. The outward part, which is connected to the senses, is subdivided into acts of worship and acts that pertain to custom. The inward part, which is connected to the states of the heart and the characteristics of the soul, is subdivided into blameworthy states and praiseworthy states. So the total makes four divisions of the sciences of the practice of religion.

The second motive [for this division] is that I have noticed the sincere interest of students in jurisprudence, which has become popular among those who do not fear God تَعَالَىٰ but who seek to boast and exploit its influence and prestige in arguments. It [jurisprudence] is also divided into four quarters, and he who follows the style of one who is beloved becomes beloved.

Translator's Introduction

بِسْمِ ٱللَّهِ ٱلرَّحْمَٰنِ ٱلرَّحِيمِ

وَالصَّلَاةُ وَالسَّلَامُ عَلَى رَسُولِهِ الْكَرِيمِ وَعَلَى آلِهِ وَأَصْحَابِهِ الطَّيِّبِيْن

إِنَّ أَوَّلَ بَيْتٍ وُضِعَ لِلنَّاسِ لَلَّذِى بِبَكَّةَ مُبَارَكًا وَهُدًى لِّلْعَٰلَمِينَ ﴿٩٦﴾ فِيهِ ءَايَٰتُۢ
بَيِّنَٰتٌ مَّقَامُ إِبْرَٰهِيمَ ۖ وَمَن دَخَلَهُۥ كَانَ ءَامِنًا ۗ وَلِلَّهِ عَلَى ٱلنَّاسِ حِجُّ ٱلْبَيْتِ مَنِ
ٱسْتَطَاعَ إِلَيْهِ سَبِيلًا ۚ وَمَن كَفَرَ فَإِنَّ ٱللَّهَ غَنِىٌّ عَنِ ٱلْعَٰلَمِينَ ﴿٩٧﴾ سُورَةُ آلِ عِمْرَان

Indeed, the first House [of worship] established for mankind was that at Mecca—blessed and a guidance for the worlds. In it are clear signs [such as] the standing place of Abraham. And whoever enters it shall be safe. And [due] to God from the people is a pilgrimage to the house—for whoever is able to find a way there. But whoever disbelieves—then indeed, God is free from need of the worlds.

Sūrat Āl-ʿImrān, 3:96–97

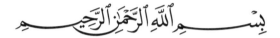

WITH book 7 of the *Revival of the Religious Sciences* (*Iḥyāʾ ʿulūm al-dīn*), Imām al-Ghazālī concludes his exposition of the five pillars of Islam with the one that most Muslims are least knowledgeable about: the pilgrimage to Mecca. For

most of the faithful, this pillar is completed just once in a lifetime. It consists of rites that are centered on the actions of the Prophet Muḥammad صَلَّى ٱللَّهُ عَلَيْهِ وَسَلَّمَ, who performed the pilgrimage once in his lifetime,[1] as well as on the actions of the Prophet Abraham عَلَيْهِ ٱلسَّلَامُ, as they commemorate events from his life. The Kaʿba itself, around which these rites take place, predates Islam. Some early commentaries on the verses quoted above state that the "first house" is but an earthly reflection of an eternal celestial house in the seventh heaven above the Kaʿba, which was first built by angels in the time of Adam عَلَيْهِ ٱلسَّلَامُ. Concerning this, al-Qurṭubī and others state that Jaʿfar al-Ṣādiq[2] رَضِيَ ٱللَّهُ عَنْهُ said:

> My father was asked in my presence concerning the origin of the sacred house and he said, "When God عَزَّ وَجَلَّ said to the angels, *Indeed, I will make upon the earth a successive authority*." *They said, "Will You place upon it one who causes corruption therein and sheds blood, while we declare Your praise and sanctify You?" God said, "Indeed, I know that which you do not know*" [2:30]. He was angered by them and they sought refuge beneath His throne and circled it seven times in hopes that He would again be content with them, and He was. Then He said to them, "Build for Me on the earth a house in which any one of the children of Adam with whom I am angry may seek refuge, and circumambulate it as you circumambulated My throne, so that I may be content with them as I am content with you." And so they built the house.[3]

This was the Kaʿba of Adam عَلَيْهِ ٱلسَّلَامُ that was eventually destroyed by the flood in the time of the Prophet Noah (Nūḥ) عَلَيْهِ ٱلسَّلَامُ. Only its foundations remained, and Abraham, hundreds of years later, was guided to it by divine revelation.[4]

---

1 According to a *ḥadīth* in Muslim and al-Bukhārī, the Prophet صَلَّى ٱللَّهُ عَلَيْهِ وَسَلَّمَ made one pilgrimage (*ḥajj*), the "pilgrimage of farewell," and four visits (*ʿumra*, pl. *ʿumar*).

2 Jaʿfar al-Ṣādiq (d. 148/765), the great-great grandson of the fourth caliph, ʿAlī (may God honor his countenance), is considered a paragon of virtue and wisdom, as well as the transmitter of numerous *ḥadīths* and legal judgments.

3 Al-Qurṭubī, *Jāmiʿ li-aḥkām al-Qurʾān*, 2:127. This is also cited by al-Suyūṭī, *al-Durr al-Manthūr*.

4 Al-Azrāqī, *Akhbār Makka*.

Of the earthly Kaʿba known to us today, the best-known history appears in a long *ḥadīth* in the collection of al-Bukhārī; it recounts the story of Abraham عَلَيْهِ ٱلسَّلَامُ, his wife Hagar (Hājar), and their infant son Ishmael (Ismāʿīl). After Sarah, Abraham's first wife, had given him her servant Hagar to take as a second wife, and after Hagar had borne him a son whom he named Ishmael, Sarah gave birth to Isaac (Isḥāq) and decided that Hagar and her baby should live elsewhere. After receiving a revelation, Abraham took them to the valley of Bakka, the oldest Arabic name for the place of the Kaʿba; this is where the story of the pilgrimage begins. The *ḥadīth* states:

> . . .[Abraham] set forth with [Hagar] and her nursing infant, Ishmael, until they reached the house, where he made a place for them under a large tree. . .[5] In those days there was no one in Mecca, nor was there any water, but he placed them there and put near them a bag of dates and a full water-skin, and then returned in the direction they had come from. The mother of Ishmael followed him and called out, "O Abraham! Where are you going? Are you leaving us in this valley with no one and nothing?" She repeated this to him several times, but he would not turn around to look at her. Then she said, "Is God the one who has commanded you to do this?" And he answered, "Yes." She replied, "Then He will not allow us to perish," and she turned back. Abraham continued to walk until he reached al-Thanīya[6] where she could no longer see him, he turned his face toward the house, and prayed: *Our Lord, I have settled some of my descendants in an uncultivated valley near Your sacred house, our Lord, that they may establish prayer. So make hearts among the people incline toward them and provide for them from the fruits that they might be grateful* [14:37].

5 This narrative seems to indicate that the house was already there, which supports the notion that a Kaʿba from Adam's time, or perhaps its remains, existed in that place. However, the narrative may also be understood to mean "the place where the house would be."

6 One of the valleys leading into Mecca. In fact, it was the same valley through which the Prophet صَلَّى ٱللَّهُ عَلَيْهِ وَسَلَّمَ entered thousands of years later.

. . .The mother of Ishmael continued to drink from the water-skin and nurse her baby until the water ran out, and then she became thirsty and her baby became thirsty as well. When she saw him in distress, she could not bear it, and so she went to the nearest hill, which was Ṣafā, climbed it, and turned toward the valley hoping to see someone, but in vain. So she came down from Ṣafā, and when she reached the bottom of the valley, she tucked up the edge of her robe and ran in desperation across the valley until she came to the hill of Marwā. She climbed it too and again looked for someone, but in vain. She repeated this course (between the two hills) seven times. Ibn ʿAbbās said that the Prophet صَلَّى ٱللَّٰهُ عَلَيْهِ وَسَلَّمَ added here, "And that is why people make the course between them."

When she reached Marwā (for the last time) she heard a voice and she told herself to be quiet and listened attentively. She heard the voice again and said, "O, (whoever you may be)! I have heard your voice; do you have something to help me?" And behold! She saw an angel at the place of Zamzam, digging the earth with his heel (or his wing), till water flowed from that place. She started to form a basin around it, using her hand in this way, and began filling her water-skin with water in her hands, and the water continued to flow after she had scooped some of it. . . The angel said to her, "Do not be afraid of being neglected, for this is the house of God which will be built by this boy and his father, and God never neglects His people."[7]

Years later, when Ishmael عَلَيْهِ ٱلسَّلَامُ was old enough to help his father build the house, Abraham made the prayer mentioned in the Qurʾān: "*Our Lord, accept* [*this*] *from us. Indeed You are the Hearing, the Knowing. Our Lord, and make us Muslims* [*in submission*] *to You and from our descendants a Muslim nation* [*in submission*] *to You. And show us our rites and accept our repentance. Indeed, You are the accepting of repentance, the Merciful* [2:127–128]. In answer to his supplication "*show us*

7 Al-Bukhārī, *Ṣaḥīḥ*, 583.

> *our rites*" [2:128], God again sent the angel Gabriel, who taught him the rituals of the pilgrimage by taking him to each place where they were to be done and physically showing him how to complete them. It is recounted in some commentaries that after each rite, the angel would ask Abraham "Do you know?" (*ʿarafta*), in the sense of "Do you understand?" and he would answer, "I know" (*ʿaraftu*), and thus the place was named *ʿarafāt* ("knowledge") and the day on which they completed the teaching of the rites came to be called *yawm al-ʿarafa* ("the day of knowing").[8]

Whatever its precise origin, it is no accident that the name of the hill and the plain on which the fourth of the four pillars of the pilgrimage is completed[9] is derived from the verb *ʿarafa* ("to know by personal experience"). As al-Ghazālī makes clear in the final part of this book, in its purest form, the pilgrimage is a journey of knowledge. In a macrocosmic sense, it reiterates the human journey to know the one God, and in a microcosmic sense, the journey of the soul to know itself and its Lord. In the pages to follow, al-Ghazālī gives us the keys to both of these journeys.

---

8 This is the Abrahamic explanation of this name, but there is also an Adamic explanation conveyed al-Ḍaḥḥāk b. Muzāḥim (d. 105/723), who said that after the fall, Adam was in India and Eve was in Jedda and they each set out in search of one another, and when they finally found each other in this sacred land of the house, "they recognized (or knew) one another" (*taʿārafā*) and so the day became known as "the day of recognition or knowing," and the place as ʿArafa (the "place of recognition"). Quoted in the commentaries on Qurʾān 2:198 of al-Baghawī, al-Thaʿlabī, al-Qurṭubī and others. For another explanation of this word, see 53 n.53.

9 On the issue of whether the pilgrimage has four or five pillars (*arkān*), see 23 n.87.

Acknowledgments

The opportunity to work on this book of the *Iḥyāʾ*, as well as on the previous four, has been a privilege for me and part of a deeply important personal journey. I would like to express my appreciation to the director of this project, Gray Henry; to Muhammad Hozien and Valerie Joy Turner for their guidance in bringing this book to fruition; and to my colleagues and friends, Fouad Aresmouk and Brahim Zoubairi, for their enormous help. Last but not least, I would like to express my eternal gratitude and love to my daughter Meriem and son-in-law Sidi Ali for taking me with them on the pilgrimage in 2002, giving me the chance to complete this pillar of faith, and allowing me to see with my own eyes at least some portion of what al-Ghazālī writes about in *Kitāb asrār al-ḥajj*. This work is dedicated to them.

THE MYSTERIES OF THE PILGRIMAGE AND ITS IMPORTANT ELEMENTS

Kitāb asrār al-ḥajj wa-muhimmātihā

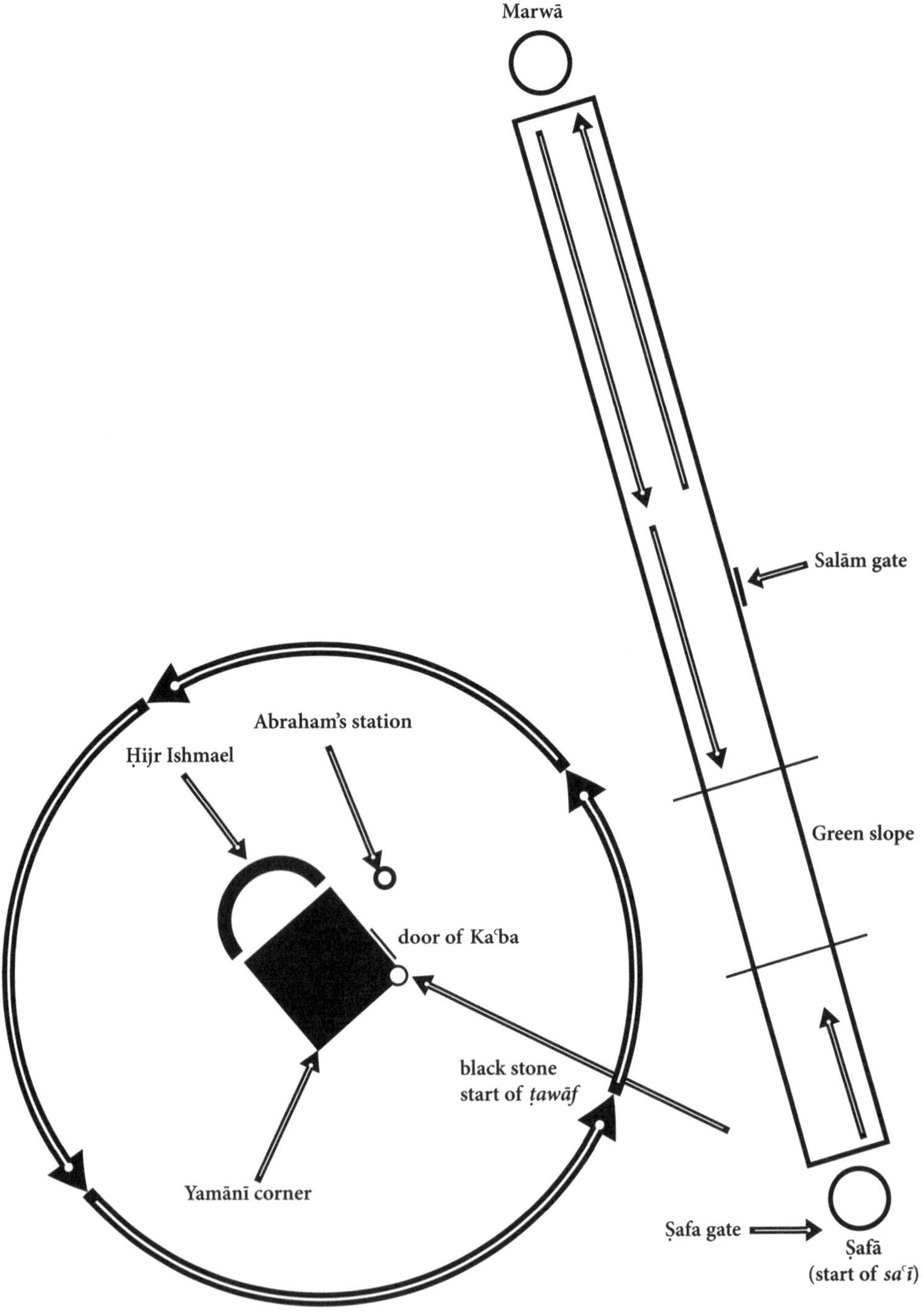

Figure 1: An approximate graphic representation of the *ḥaram* area showing the Kaʿba and landmarks discussed in the text. These are not to scale.

[al-Ghazālī's Introduction]

In the Name of God, the Merciful and Compassionate

The Mysteries of the Pilgrimage and Its Important Elements

Book 7 of the *Revival of the Religious Sciences*

PRAISE be to God who made the testimony of His unity a protection and a citadel for His servants and made the ancient house a place of gathering and a sanctuary and then endowed it with a special relationship to Himself as an honor, a fortification, and a benefaction, and made visiting it and circumambulating it a veil and shield between the servant and the chastisement of the hereafter.

And may blessings be on Muḥammad, the Prophet of mercy and the master of the community, and on his family and Companions, leaders of the truth and the best of humankind—may blessings be on them all and salutations of peace in abundance.

To proceed: The pilgrimage is among the pillars of Islam and its foundations, the worship of a lifetime and its seal, the completion of Islam and perfection of *dīn*.[1] In it, God عَزَّوَجَلَّ revealed to the Prophet صَلَّىٱللَّهُعَلَيْهِوَسَلَّمَ,

ٱلْيَوْمَ أَكْمَلْتُ لَكُمْ دِينَكُمْ وَأَتْمَمْتُ عَلَيْكُمْ نِعْمَتِي وَرَضِيتُ لَكُمُ ٱلْإِسْلَٰمَ دِينًا ۚ ۝٣

This day I have perfected for you your dīn and completed My favor upon you and have approved for you Islam as dīn [5:3].

1 *Dīn*, often translated as "religion," more accurately means a way of life based on belief, devotion, and virtue.

Concerning this act of worship, the Prophet ﷺ said, "Whoever dies and has not made the pilgrimage—he should die as either a Jew or a Christian, whichever he wants."[2]

How great, then, is an act of worship without which the *dīn* is incomplete, such that one who fails to complete it [without excuse] becomes equal to a Jew or Christian in misguidance, and how deserving of an effort to explain it, to detail its pillars, its *sunna* elements, its manners, merits, and mysteries.

All this will be revealed with the help of God عَزَّوَجَلَّ, in three chapters.

The first concerns the merits [of the pilgrimage], Mecca, and the ancient house, and includes its pillars, conditions, and obligatory aspects.

The second concerns its outward actions and the order in which they occur, from the beginning of the journey until the return.

The third chapter concerns the details of its manners, subtle mysteries, and inward practices.

Let us begin with the first chapter.

2 Al-Tirmidhī, *Sunan*, 812; al-Dārimī, *Sunan*, 1826; Abū Nuʿaym, *Ḥilya*, 9:201; al-Bayhaqī, *al-Sunan al-kubrā*, 4:334.

1

On the Merits of the Pilgrimage, Mecca, and the Ancient House, Including Its Pillars, Conditions, and Obligations

Section 1: On the Merits of the Pilgrimage, the House, and Mecca and Medina, May God Protect Them, and of Visiting the [Three] Sacred Sites[1]

The Merits of the Pilgrimage

God عَزَّوَجَلَّ says:

وَأَذِّن فِي ٱلنَّاسِ بِٱلْحَجِّ يَأْتُوكَ رِجَالًا وَعَلَىٰ كُلِّ ضَامِرٍ يَأْتِينَ مِن كُلِّ فَجٍّ عَمِيقٍ ﴿٢٧﴾

And proclaim to the people the ḥajj [pilgrimage]; they will come to you on foot and on every lean camel; they will come from every distant pass [22:27].

[Commenting on this] Qatāda said, "When God عَزَّوَجَلَّ commanded Abraham عَلَيْهِ السَّلَامُ to proclaim to mankind the pilgrimage, he called out, "O you people! God تَعَالَىٰ has a house, so make pilgrimage to it."[2]

And God تَعَالَىٰ says [of the pilgrimage],

1 By which is meant Mecca, Medina, and Jerusalem.

2 This was narrated by Qatāda from ʿIkrima b. Khālid, as found in Ibn Abī ʿArūba, *Manāsik*, 22; Ibn ʿAsākir, *Tārīkh madinat Dimashq*, 6:207.

لِّيَشْهَدُواْ مَنَـٰفِعَ لَهُمْ ٢٨

That they may witness benefits for themselves [22:28],

which is said to mean, "Trade that takes place during those months and recompense in the hereafter."[3]

One of the early believers, on hearing this verse, said, "By the Lord of the Kaʿba! [It is so] they might be forgiven their sins!"[4]

And it has been said in explanation of the words of God عَزَّوَجَلَّ,

قَالَ فَبِمَآ أَغْوَيْتَنِي لَأَقْعُدَنَّ لَهُمْ صِرَٰطَكَ ٱلْمُسْتَقِيمَ ١٦

[*Satan*] *said, "Because You have put me in error, I will surely sit in wait for them on Your straight path"* [7:16],

that this means the path to Mecca, where Satan lies in ambush to prevent people from [making the pilgrimage].[5]

The Prophet صَلَّىٱللَّهُعَلَيْهِوَسَلَّمَ said, "Whoever performs the pilgrimage to the house and avoids any obscenity or lewdness [in the course of it] will emerge from his sins as pure as on the day his mother bore him."[6]

And he said صَلَّىٱللَّهُعَلَيْهِوَسَلَّمَ, "Satan is never seen smaller, more humiliated, more despised, and more furious than on the day of ʿArafa." And this is only because he sees how God's mercy descends on that day and how many major sins God forgives, even as it has been said, "There are some sins for which only standing at ʿArafa is expiation." Jaʿfar b. Muḥammad attributes this saying to the Messenger صَلَّىٱللَّهُعَلَيْهِوَسَلَّمَ of God.[7]

One of the people of insight from those near God said that Iblīs once appeared to him at ʿArafa in the form of a person [who was] physically weak, jaundiced, weeping, and with a broken back.

The man said to him, "Why are your eyes full of tears?"

---

3 According to Mujāhid as recorded by al-Ṭabarī in his *Tafsīr*, 10:17:186.

4 Abū Ṭālib al-Makkī, *Qūt al-qulūb*, 2:120.

5 Abū Nuʿaym, *Ḥilya*, 4:253. This narration can also be traced back to ʿAbdallāh b. Masʿūd رَضِيَٱللَّهُعَنْهُ in al-Fākihī, *Akhbār Makka*, 4:132.

6 Al-Bukhārī, *Ṣaḥīḥ*, 1521; Muslim, *Ṣaḥīḥ*, 1350.

7 Abū Ṭālib al-Makkī, *Qūt al-qulūb*, 2:120.

> He [Iblīs] answered, "Because of these pilgrims going forth with no thought of commerce. Their only goal is the pilgrimage and I am afraid they will not fail to reach it! That is what makes me miserable."
>
> Then the man asked him, "And what has made your body so frail?"
>
> And [Iblīs] answered, "The whinnying of horses [ridden] for the sake of God عَزَّوَجَلَّ. If it were for my sake, I would love it more!"
>
> Then he [the man] asked, "And what has changed your color?"
>
> And he [Iblīs] answered, "A community of people helping one another to obey God. If they were helping one another toward sin, I would love it more!"
>
> Then he [the man] asked, "And what has broken your back?"
>
> And he [Iblīs] answered, "When the servant says: 'O God, I ask You for a good ending,' I say, 'Woe to me! When will this man become deluded by his own deeds?' And I fear that he has become aware [of the danger of self-reliance]!"[8]

The Prophet صَلَّى ٱللَّهُ عَلَيْهِ وَسَلَّمَ said,

> For whoever sets out from his home for the pilgrimage or the visit (*ʿumra*)[9] and dies, the reward will be that of the pilgrimage and the visit [made every year] until the day of resurrection. And whoever dies in one of the two sacred mosques will not be exposed nor reckoned [on the plain of the resurrection] and it will be said to him: enter heaven.[10]

---

8 Abū Ṭālib al-Makkī, *Qūt al-qulūb*, 2:120. A *ḥadīth* with a similar meaning appears in Ibn Mājah, *Sunan*, 3013. The last two parts of this anecdote mean that a servant should not become so satisfied with his devotional practices that he depends on these acts instead of on the mercy of God.

9 The *ʿumra* ("visit" or lesser pilgrimage) is a voluntary pilgrimage to Mecca. See, p. 71.

10 Al-Ṭabarānī, *al-Muʿjam al-awsaṭ*, 5374; al-Bayhaqī, *Shuʿab al-īmān*, 3802.

And he صَلَّى ٱللَّٰهُ عَلَيْهِ وَسَلَّمَ said "An accepted pilgrimage is better than the world and all it contains. An accepted pilgrimage has no recompense other than heaven."[11]

And he صَلَّى ٱللَّٰهُ عَلَيْهِ وَسَلَّمَ said, "Those who go on the pilgrimage or the visit are God's delegation and His visitors. If they ask of Him, He gives to them. If they seek His forgiveness, He forgives them. If they call Him, He answers them. If they seek intercession [for another], their intercession is granted."[12]

And in a *ḥadīth* whose chain of transmission is to the family of the Prophet صَلَّى ٱللَّٰهُ عَلَيْهِ وَسَلَّمَ, it is stated: "The most sinful of people is someone who stands at ʿArafa and thinks that God تَعَالَىٰ will not forgive him."[13]

According to Ibn ʿAbbās رَضِيَ ٱللَّٰهُ عَنْهُمَا, the Prophet صَلَّى ٱللَّٰهُ عَلَيْهِ وَسَلَّمَ said, "Every day there descends on this house [complex] one hundred twenty portions of God's mercy. Sixty for those making *ṭawāf* around it, forty for those praying, and twenty for those who are gazing at it."[14]

And another narration states, "Increase [your] circumambulations of the house, for it will be among the greatest acts and most precious deeds you will find recorded for you on the day of resurrection."[15] For this reason it is a recommended practice to do the circumambulation (*ṭawāf*)[16] first [when visiting Mecca], even apart from during the pilgrimage and visit.

Yet another [narration] states, "The reward of someone who makes a circumambulation around the Kaʿba seven times, barefoot and bareheaded, is as if he had freed a slave, and whoever does this seven times in the rain is forgiven all his past sins."[17]

---

11 Al-Bukhārī, *Ṣaḥīḥ*, 1773; Muslim, *Ṣaḥīḥ*, 1349, beginning with the words, "The lesser pilgrimage (*ʿumra*) to the lesser pilgrimage is expiation for the sins that are committed between them…"

12 Abū Ṭālib al-Makkī, *Qūt al-qulūb*, 2:120. A similar saying appears in Ibn Mājah, *Sunan*, 2892.

13 Abū Ṭālib al-Makkī, *Qūt al-qulūb*, 2:120; al-Khaṭīb al-Baghdādī, *al-Muttafiq wa-l-muftariqu*, 219.

14 Al-Ṭabarānī, *al-Muʿjam al-kabīr*, 11:195; Abū Nuʿaym, *Tārīkh Iṣbahān*, 1:151.

15 Abū Ṭālib al-Makkī, *Qūt al-qulūb*, 2:119; al-Azraqī, *Akhbār Makka*, 1:218.

16 Henceforth, we use the word 'circumambulation' and *ṭawāf* interchangeably.

17 Abū Ṭālib al-Makkī, *Qūt al-qulūb*, 2:119. The first part of this *ḥadīth* appears in al-Tirmidhī, *Sunan*, 959, and a similar *ḥadīth* on circumambulation (*ṭawāf*) in the rain appears in Ibn Mājah, *Sunan*, 1401, 3118.

And it is said, "Whenever God عَزَّوَجَلَّ forgives a sin of His servant during the standing [at ʿArafa], He forgives all the others standing [at ʿArafa] who have committed that [same] sin."[18]

One of the early believers said, "If the day of ʿArafa is on a Friday, all who stand at ʿArafa are forgiven their sins,"[19] for this is the most excellent day in this world. It was on such a day that the Messenger صَلَّىٱللَّهُعَلَيْهِوَسَلَّمَ of God completed his farewell pilgrimage, and he was standing [at ʿArafa] when the words of God تَعَالَىٰ were revealed to him:

ٱلْيَوْمَ أَكْمَلْتُ لَكُمْ دِينَكُمْ وَأَتْمَمْتُ عَلَيْكُمْ نِعْمَتِي
وَرَضِيتُ لَكُمُ ٱلْإِسْلَٰمَ دِينًاۚ ﴿٣﴾

This day I have perfected for you your dīn and completed My favor upon you and have approved for you Islam as dīn [5:3].

The people of the Book said, "Had this verse been revealed to us, we would have made it a day of feast (*ʿīd*)." And ʿUmar رَضِيَٱللَّهُعَنْهُ said, "I testify that this verse was revealed on a day of two feasts—the day of ʿArafa and Friday [the day of the assembly]—and the Messenger صَلَّىٱللَّهُعَلَيْهِوَسَلَّمَ of God was standing at ʿArafa at the time."[20]

The Prophet صَلَّىٱللَّهُعَلَيْهِوَسَلَّمَ said, "O God, forgive the pilgrim and the man for whom the pilgrim asks forgiveness."[21]

It has been reported that ʿAlī b. Muwaffaq performed several pilgrimages on behalf of the Messenger صَلَّىٱللَّهُعَلَيْهِوَسَلَّمَ of God.

> He [ʿAlī] said, "I saw the Messenger صَلَّىٱللَّهُعَلَيْهِوَسَلَّمَ of God in a dream and he [the Prophet صَلَّىٱللَّهُعَلَيْهِوَسَلَّمَ] said to me, 'O Ibn Muwaffaq, have you performed pilgrimages on my behalf?'"
>
> I [ʿAlī] said, 'Yes.'
>
> Then he [the Prophet صَلَّىٱللَّهُعَلَيْهِوَسَلَّمَ] asked, 'And did you repeat *labbayka*[22] on my behalf?'

---

18 Abū Ṭālib al-Makkī, *Qūt al-qulūb*, 2:120.
19 Abū Ṭālib al-Makkī, *Qūt al-qulūb*, 2:120.
20 Al-Bukhārī, *Ṣaḥīḥ*, 45; Muslim, *Ṣaḥīḥ*, 3017.
21 Al-Ṭabarānī, *al-Muʿjam al-awsaṭ*, 8589; al-Ḥākim al-Nīsābūrī, *al-Mustadrak*, 1:441.
22 That is, the pilgrim's invocation (*talbiyya*); see p. 37.

> I [ʿAlī] replied, 'Yes.'
>
> He [the Prophet ﷺ] said, 'Then I shall return this goodness to you on the day of resurrection. I will take you by the hand in the place of standing and bring you into heaven while all the people are going through the ordeal of the reckoning.'"[23]

Mujāhid and other scholars said, "When pilgrims reach Mecca, they are met by angels who greet those who ride on camels, shake the hand of those who ride on donkeys, and embrace those who walk on foot."[24]

Ḥasan said, "Whoever dies following Ramaḍān, or following a battle, or following the pilgrimage dies as a martyr."[25]

And ʿUmar رَضِيَ ٱللَّٰهُ عَنْهُ said, "The pilgrim is forgiven his sins as well as those of anyone for whom he asks forgiveness during the months of Dhū l-Ḥijja, Muḥarram, Ṣafar, and ten [days] of Rabīʿ al-Awwal."[26]

It was the custom of the early believers رَضِيَ ٱللَّٰهُ عَنْهُمْ to bid farewell to those departing for battle and to welcome back those returning from pilgrimage; [they would] kiss them between the eyes and ask them for their prayers, and they would hasten to do this before they became tainted by sin.[27]

ʿAlī b. Muwaffaq is reported to have said,

> I performed the pilgrimage one year, and when it was the night of ʿArafa I slept in the mosque of al-Khayf at Minā and saw in a dream that two angels clothed in green descended from the sky.
>
> Then one of them called out to the other, "O servant of God!" and the other replied, "Here I am! (*labbayka*) O servant of God!"
>
> The first then asked, "Do you know how many performed the pilgrimage to the house of our Lord عَزَّ وَجَلَّ this year?"
>
> And the second answered, "I do not know."

23 Abū Ṭālib al-Makkī, *Qūt al-qulūb*, 2:121.

24 Al-Bayhaqī, *Shuʿab al-īmān*, 3805; al-Fākihī, *Akhbār Makka*, 2:276.

25 Abū Ṭālib al-Makkī, *Qūt al-qulūb*, 2:120.

26 Abū Ṭālib al-Makkī, *Qūt al-qulūb*, 2:120.

27 Abū Ṭālib al-Makkī, *Qūt al-qulūb*, 2:120.

The first then said, "Six hundred thousand have performed the pilgrimage to the house of our Lord! And do you know how many of them were accepted?"

And the other answered, "No," and the first said, "Only six."

He [ʿAlī b. Muwaffaq] continued, "Then they ascended into the air and disappeared from me, and I woke up frightened and full of woe and distress about my state. I said to myself, if the pilgrimage of only six people has been accepted, how can I ever be among those six?"

After I left ʿArafa, I remained for a while in the sacred precincts, and [one day] as I was reflecting on the multitude of people [who made the pilgrimage] and the small number who are accepted, I fell asleep, and there were the two beings again, who descended in the same forms I had seen before. One of them called out to the other and repeated precisely the same words [I had heard before] and then said, "Do you know what our Lord عَزَّوَجَلَّ has decreed this night?" The other said, "No," and he [the first] said, "For each of the six, he has accepted one hundred thousand [others]."

He [Ibn Muwwafaq] said, "And I awoke with a joy beyond description."[28]

It is also related that he [Ibn Muwwafaq] رَضِيَ ٱللَّهُ عَنْهُ said,

I performed the pilgrimage one year and when I completed the rites I began thinking about those whose pilgrimage had not been accepted and I said, "O God, I donate my pilgrimage and its reward to someone whose pilgrimage was not accepted." Then I saw the Lord of honor عَزَّوَجَلَّ in my sleep, and He said to me, "O ʿAlī, are you [claiming to be] more generous than I, when I am the One who created generosity and benevolence, and I am the most generous of the generous, the most benevolent of the benevolent, and the more deserving of the attribute of generosity and benevolence than anyone in creation? For this I have bestowed on all those whose pilgrimages were not accepted the pilgrimages of those who were!"

28 Abū Ṭālib al-Makkī, *Qūt al-qulūb*, 2:120.

The Merits of the House and Mecca, May God Protect It

The Prophet صَلَّى ٱللَّٰهُ عَلَيْهِ وَسَلَّمَ said,

> God عَزَّ وَجَلَّ promised that every year six hundred thousand will make pilgrimages to it [this house], and if this number falls short, He will complete it with angels. And [He promised] that they will crowd around the Kaʿba like a bride in a wedding procession, and they will cling to the curtains and hasten around it until it enters heaven and they enter along with it.[29]

And a tradition states, "The black stone is a gem from one of the gemstones of paradise. It will be raised up on the day of resurrection with eyes and a tongue with which it will speak, bearing witness to all those who greeted it properly and sincerely."[30]

The Prophet صَلَّى ٱللَّٰهُ عَلَيْهِ وَسَلَّمَ used to kiss it a lot[31] and it is reported that he prostrated himself before it[32] and made *ṭawāf* on a camel, touched it with his camel stick, and then kissed the end of the stick.[33]

> ʿUmar رَضِيَ ٱللَّٰهُ عَنْهُ once kissed the black stone and then said, "I know you are a stone and that you cannot cause harm or benefit, and if I had not seen the Messenger صَلَّى ٱللَّٰهُ عَلَيْهِ وَسَلَّمَ of God kiss you, I would not have done it."
>
> Then he wept until his sobbing grew loud, and he turned around and saw ʿAlī, may God honor his countenance and be pleased with him, who said, "O Abū l-Ḥasan, this is a place where tears must flow."
>
> ʿAlī said, "O Commander of the Faithful, it does indeed cause harm and benefit."
>
> ʿUmar said, "How?"

---

29 Abū Ṭālib al-Makkī, *Qūt al-qulūb*, 2:121; al-Fākihī, *Akhbār Makka*, 1:436. A related saying recounted in al-Suyūṭī, *al-Durr al-manthūr*, 1:329, states, "The hour will not arise until the Kaʿba is taken as if in a procession to the sacred mosque of Jerusalem and they will lead their people into heaven, but the day of exposition and reckoning will take place in the sacred mosque."

30 Al-Tirmidhī, *Sunan*, 961, with wording similar to this.

31 The Prophet's kissing of the black stone is mentioned in al-Bukhārī, *Ṣaḥīḥ*, 1597; Muslim, *Ṣaḥīḥ*, 1270.

32 Al-Dāraquṭnī, *Sunan*, 2:289; al-Ḥākim al-Nīsābūrī, *al-Mustadrak*, 1:473.

33 Muslim, *Ṣaḥīḥ*, 1275.

> And [ʿAlī] said, "When God تَعَالَىٰ made a covenant with the children [of Adam], He recorded [it] for them in writing and then placed it in this rock that it might bear witness that the believer fulfilled the covenant and bear witness that the unbeliever did not."[34]

It is said that this is the meaning of those words spoken by people on touching [the black stone], "O God, [I do this] believing in You, affirming the truth of Your book, and fulfilling Your covenant."[35] It is related from Ḥasan al-Baṣrī رَضِيَ اللَّهُ عَنْهُ that one day of fasting [in Mecca] is equal to one hundred thousand days of fasting [elsewhere], one dirham given as charity [in Mecca] is equal to one hundred thousand dirhams [given elsewhere], and likewise every act of goodness is one hundred thousand times [more excellent there].[36]

And it is said that seven circumambulations (*ṭawāf*) of seven [rounds each] are equal to the visit (*ʿumra*), and that three visits are equal to one pilgrimage.[37]

A sound tradition states: "Making the visit (*ʿumra*) in Ramaḍān is like performing the pilgrimage with me."[38]

And he صَلَّىٰ اللَّهُ عَلَيْهِ وَسَلَّمَ said,

> I am the first on whom the earth will split open [on the day of resurrection]. Then I will go to the people in al-Baqīʿ[39] and they will be resurrected with me. Then I will go to the people of Mecca and we will be resurrected between the two sanctuaries (*ḥaramayn*).[40]

In another narrative, he صَلَّىٰ اللَّهُ عَلَيْهِ وَسَلَّمَ said, "When Adam عَلَيْهِ السَّلَامُ was completing the rites [of the pilgrimage], he was met by the angels, who said to him, 'May your pilgrimage be accepted, O

---

34 Abū Ṭālib al-Makkī, *Qūt al-qulūb*, 2:121; al-Azraqī, *Akhbār Makka*, 1:257.

35 This supplication, which commonly begins with "In the name of God, God is greater..." was well-known among the early believers and is related in numerous sources.

36 Abū Ṭālib al-Makkī, *Qūt al-qulūb*, 2:121.

37 Abū Ṭālib al-Makkī, *Qūt al-qulūb*, 2:120.

38 Al-Bukhārī, *Ṣaḥīḥ*, 1782; Muslim, *Ṣaḥīḥ*, 1256.

39 Al-Baqīʿ is the cemetery in Medina where many of the Companions and the people of the Prophet's family are buried.

40 Al-Tirmidhī, *Sunan*, 3692.

Adam! Verily we made the pilgrimage to this house two thousand years before you!'"[41]

Another tradition states,

> God تَعَالَىٰ looks on the people of the earth each night. The first of those on whom He looks are the people of the sanctuary (*ḥaram*), and the first of the people of the sanctuary on whom He looks are the people in the sacred mosque. Anyone He sees performing the *ṭawāf*, He forgives, and anyone He sees praying, He forgives, and even the ones He sees sleeping with their faces toward the *qibla*, He forgives.[42]

One of the friends رَضِيَ ٱللَّهُ عَنْهُ [of God] had a vision. He said, "I saw all the frontier regions prostrate themselves before ʿAbbādān, and I saw ʿAbbādān prostrate itself before Judda [Jedda]."[43]

It is also said that the sun does not set on any day without one of the *abdāl* making *ṭawāf* of this house, nor does dawn break from the night without one of the *awtād* making *ṭawāf*.[44] If this were to cease, it would cause the Kaʿba to be taken from the earth, such that people would awaken one morning and find not a trace of it left. Indeed, this is what will happen when seven years pass by without anyone making the pilgrimage. Then [in that case], the Qurʾān will

41 Al-Azraqī, *Akhbār Makka*, 1:16; al-Bayhaqī, *Shuʿab al-īmān*, 3703.

42 Abū Ṭālib al-Makkī, *Qūt al-qulūb*, 2:121.

43 Abū Ṭālib al-Makkī, *Qūt al-qulūb*, 2:121. "ʿAbbādān" is the former name of the region in the south of present-day Iraq. "Judda" is the traditional pronunciation of present-day Jedda.

44 The *abdāl* (substitutes) and *awtād* (stakes) are the highest rank of saints. The terms appear in a *ḥadīth* quoted in al-Ḥakīm al-Tirmidhī, *Nawādir al-uṣūl* 1:262, where their number is mentioned as thirty or forty. In the context of the *ḥadīth*, they are called "substitutes" because whenever one of them dies, another is substituted in his or her place, or they are called "stakes" because they "hold" the earth in its place. The latter term also appears in the Qurʾān: ... *and the mountains as stakes* **(78:7)**. Al-Ghazālī refers to the *abdāl* in the Quarter of Perils, Book 29, *The Censure of Pride and Vanity* (*Iḥyāʾ*, 6:535). Sufis believe in ranks in a spiritual hierarchy of saints or mystics that lived after the time of the Prophet. These saints are said to be unknown to the generality of believers, but have a powerful influence in preserving the order of the universe. Some Sufi texts present this hierarchy as follows: at the apex there is an axis or pole (*quṭb*), the axis mundi or spiritual pole of the universe. After the pole are the two foremost or assistants (*imāmān*); below them are five mainstays (*awtād*), or pillars (*ʿumud*); then seven incomparables (*afrād*); then the substitutes (*abdāl*); and so on for ten ranks in total. See al-Tustarī, *Tafsīr al-Tustarī*, trans. Keeler and Keeler, 89 n.5.

be lifted from the books (*al-maṣāḥif*) and people will awaken to find the pages stark white without a single letter. Then the Qurʾān will be removed from people's hearts, such that not a word of it will be remembered. Then people will revert to the poetry, songs, and tales of the *jāhiliyya*,[45] the Antichrist [al-Masīḥ al-Dajjāl] will emerge, and Jesus عَلَيْهِ ٱلسَّلَامُ will descend [from heaven] and kill him. The hour when this occurs will be like a pregnant woman in labor, waiting for the moment of her delivery.[46]

It is said in a tradition, "Increase circumambulations (*ṭawāf*) of this house before it is raised up, for it has been destroyed twice and on the third occasion it will be raised up."[47]

And it is related from ʿAlī رَضِيَ ٱللَّهُ عَنْهُ that the Prophet صَلَّى ٱللَّهُ عَلَيْهِ وَسَلَّمَ said, "God تَعَالَىٰ said, 'If I wished to destroy the world, I would begin by destroying My house and then destroy the world in its wake.'"[48]

The Merits of Residing in Mecca *mukarrama*, May God Protect It, and [the Reasons for] Disapproving of It

The more cautious scholars disapprove of residing in Mecca for three reasons.

First is the fear that someone will become bored with being there and become so familiar with the house that the fervor in the heart will be extinguished. Thus ʿUmar رَضِيَ ٱللَّهُ عَنْهُ would strike the pilgrims who had finished the rites, saying, "O you people of Yemen, back to Yemen with you! O you people of Syria, back to Syria with you! O you people of Iraq, back to Iraq with you!"[49] Also for this reason ʿUmar رَضِيَ ٱللَّهُ عَنْهُ forbade people from making too many

45 Literally, "time of ignorance," generally used to refer to the period in Arabia before Islam.

46 Abū Ṭālib al-Makkī, *Qūt al-qulūb*, 2:121.

47 This tradition is a reminder for Muslims to seize the opportunity to earn more reward, because access to the sacred precinct is not always assured (e.g, in times of outbreak of disease). Ibn Ḥibbān, *Ṣaḥīḥ*, 2753; al-Ḥākim al-Nīsābūrī, *al-Mustadrak*, 1:441.

48 Abū Ṭālib al-Makkī, *Qūt al-qulūb*, 2:122. The destruction of the Kaʿba at the end of time is mentioned in al-Bukhārī, *Ṣaḥīḥ*, 1091; Muslim, *Ṣaḥīḥ*, 2909.

49 Abū Ṭālib al-Makkī, *Qūt al-qulūb*, 2:122; and with similar meaning in Ibn Abī Shayba, *al-Muṣannaf*, 13470.

circumambulations (*ṭawāf*), saying, "I am afraid they will become too familiar with the house."

Second, separation gives rise to yearning and a motive to return. As the Qurʾān states, God تَعَالَىٰ says, I made the house a place of return for the people and [a place of] security,[50] meaning, a place where they assemble time after time but never stop desiring [to revisit it].

One [of the scholars] said, "It is better to be in some other land with your heart yearning for Mecca and attached to this house than to be in [Mecca] bored with your stay, with your heart in another land."[51]

And one of the early believers said, "How many a man in Khurāsān is nearer to this house than someone who might be making *ṭawāf* around it."[52]

It is also said that God تَعَالَىٰ has servants who are so near Him that the Kaʿba makes *ṭawāf* around them.[53]

Third is the fear that [while residing there] someone might commit transgressions and sins and in that there is a danger, considering the nobility of the place, of bringing the wrath of God عَزَّوَجَلَّ on oneself.

Wuhayb b. al-Ward al-Makkī is reported to have said, "One night I was praying in Ḥijr[54] when I heard a voice between the Kaʿba and the curtain say, 'To God I complain, then to you, O Gabriel, of what comes from those who make circumambulations (*ṭawāf*) around me, engrossed in chatter, and vain prattle. If they do not cease, I

50 This is an allusion to the Qurʾān, *a place of return for the people and [a place of] security* [2:125] and *Have they not seen that We made [Mecca] a safe sanctuary, while people are being taken away all around them?* [29:67]. Traditionally Meccans, even in the time before Islam, offered all those who worship at the Kaʿba a sanctuary, especially during the pilgrimage season. So those seeking relative safety always found it a place of security. This continued into the modern period. The caliph's role was not only to safeguard the pilgrims, but also the pilgrimage routes. See al-Ṭabarī, *Tafsīr*

51 Abū Ṭālib al-Makkī, *Qūt al-qulūb*, 2:122.

52 Abū Ṭālib al-Makkī, *Qūt al-qulūb*, 2:122; Ibn Abī Shayba, *al-Muṣannaf*, 13470.

53 Abū Ṭālib al-Makkī, *Qūt al-qulūb*, 2:122; see also al-Ālūsī, *Tafsīr*, 23:14–15.

54 Ḥijr Ishmael, also referred to as al-Ḥaṭīm, is presently marked by a semi-circle of marble. It is considered to be the place where Abraham عَلَيْهِ السَّلَامُ built a shelter for his wife Hagar and baby Ishmael and is also thought to have been part of the original Kaʿba. For that reason, *ṭawāf* must be done outside this structure, as explained below.

will quake with such a quaking that every stone in me will return to the mountain from which it was cut."[55]

Ibn Masʿūd رَضِيَ اللَّهُ عَنْهُ said, "There is no land in which a servant can incur retribution for even thinking about doing wrong before actually doing it, except Mecca," and then he recited the words of [God] تَعَالَىٰ

وَمَن يُرِدْ فِيهِ بِإِلْحَادٍۭ بِظُلْمٍ نُّذِقْهُ مِنْ عَذَابٍ أَلِيمٍ ﴿٢٥﴾

and [*also*] *whoever intends* [*a deed*] *therein of deviation* [*in religion*] *or wrongdoing—We will make him taste a painful punishment* [22:25].[56]

It is also said that bad deeds are multiplied [in Mecca], just as good deeds are.[57]

Ibn ʿAbbās رَضِيَ اللَّهُ عَنْهُمَا used to say, "To hoard [food in an effort to drive the price up] in the sanctuary of Mecca is an act of apostasy."[58]

And the same is said of lying.[59]

Ibn ʿAbbās also said, "To commit seventy sins in Rukba is preferable to me than committing one in Mecca." Rukba is a stopping place between Mecca and Taif.[60]

Fearing this, some of those who reside [in Mecca] leave the sanctuary for the surrounding hills when they have to answer the call of nature. And there was also a man among them who spent a month without even lying down on his side on the ground.

Some scholars ruled that to receive payment for [renting] one of its houses is a practice that is disapproved of; this is also in order to prevent people from staying in [Mecca].[61]

Let it not be supposed, however, that this disapproval of residing [in Mecca] contradicts the excellence of that land. The disapproval arises from people's weakness and inability to live up to the sanctity of the place. If we say "it is preferable not to reside there," we mean,

55 Al-Azraqī, *Akhbār Makka*, 2:13.

56 Al-Azraqī, *Akhbār Makka*, 2:13.

57 Al-Azraqī, *Akhbār Makka*, 2:13.

58 Abū Ṭālib al-Makkī, *Qūt al-qulūb*, 2:119; al-Azraqī, *Akhbār Makka*, 2:126.

59 Abū Ṭālib al-Makkī, *Qūt al-qulūb*, 2:119

60 Al-Zabīdī, *Itḥāf*, 4:282, notes that Ibn ʿAbbās camped the night there when traveling between Mecca and Taif.

61 Al-Fākihī, *Akhbār Makka*, 3:247.

because of our shortcomings and susceptibility to boredom; but with regard to staying there while fulfilling what is due—how could there be anything better? How could it be otherwise, when the Messenger صَلَّى ٱللَّٰهُ عَلَيْهِ وَسَلَّمَ of God returned to Mecca, faced the Kaʿba, and said, "You are the best place on God's earth! You are the most beloved land to me! If I had not been made to leave you, I would never have left you!"[62] And how could it be otherwise when [merely] looking at the sacred house is [considered] worship, and the good deeds in it are rewarded many times over, as we mentioned?

The Excellence of the City of the Messenger صَلَّى ٱللَّٰهُ عَلَيْهِ وَسَلَّمَ of God over All Other Lands

AFTER Mecca, there is no place more excellent than Medina, [the city] of the Messenger صَلَّى ٱللَّٰهُ عَلَيْهِ وَسَلَّمَ of God. [Good] deeds completed there are also multiplied, just as [in Mecca], and the Prophet صَلَّى ٱللَّٰهُ عَلَيْهِ وَسَلَّمَ said, "One prayer in this, my mosque, is better than one thousand prayers anywhere else, except in the sacred mosque."[63]

Similarly, every [good] deed done in Medina is multiplied one thousandfold. After Medina comes the holy land [Jerusalem], where every prayer is [equal to] five hundred prayers elsewhere, and this is the case with all other deeds. Ibn ʿAbbās reported that the Prophet صَلَّى ٱللَّٰهُ عَلَيْهِ وَسَلَّمَ said, "A prayer in the mosque of Medina is [equal to] ten thousand prayers, and a prayer in al-Masjid al-Aqṣā [in Jerusalem] is [equal to] one thousand prayers, and a prayer in the sacred mosque [of Mecca] is [equal to] one hundred thousand prayers.[64]

He صَلَّى ٱللَّٰهُ عَلَيْهِ وَسَلَّمَ [also] said, "No one endures the hardships and severity of Medina except that I will be his intercessor on the day of resurrection."[65]

---

62 Al-Tirmidhī, *Sunan*, 3925; Ibn Mājah, *Sunan*, 3108.

63 Al-Bukhārī, *Ṣaḥīḥ*, 1190; Muslim, *Ṣaḥīḥ*, 1394.

64 Abū Ṭālib al-Makkī, *Qūt al-qulūb*, 2:123. A *ḥadīth* with the same meaning can be found in Ibn Mājah, *Sunan*, 1407.

65 Muslim, *Ṣaḥīḥ*, 1363.

He صَلَّى ٱللَّهُ عَلَيْهِ وَسَلَّمَ [also] said, "Anyone who is able to die in Medina should do so [there], for no one dies there except that I will be his intercessor on the day of resurrection."[66]

After these three sacred places, all others are equal except for the frontiers, where staying for the sake of defense has great merit. Thus, he صَلَّى ٱللَّهُ عَلَيْهِ وَسَلَّمَ said, "Do not set out on a journey to [any place] but these three mosques: the sacred mosque [Mecca], my mosque [Medina], and al-Masjid al-Aqṣā [Jerusalem]."[67]

Certain scholars have taken this *ḥadīth* as proof for the prohibition of traveling to visit the shrines of the saints or the tombs of great scholars, but this does not appear to me to be the case, rather visiting [tombs] was, in fact, commanded by what he صَلَّى ٱللَّهُ عَلَيْهِ وَسَلَّمَ said, "I used to forbid you from visiting tombs, [but now I am telling you to] visit them and do not speak ill [of them]."[68]

In truth, the *ḥadīth* in question concerns mosques and not the meaning of tombs. With the exception of the three mentioned, all mosques are the same, and since there is no town without a mosque in it, there is no sense in setting out on a journey to another mosque. Tombs, however, are not the same, and the blessing (*baraka*) that may come from visiting them depends on their rank with God عَزَّ وَجَلَّ.

Of course, if someone [lived] in a place where there is no mosque, then he should set off for a place where there is a mosque, and even move there permanently if he so desires.

I wonder, as well, whether the one who proclaims [that such visits are prohibited] would also prohibit people from making journeys to the tombs of the prophets عَلَيْهِمُ ٱلسَّلَامُ, such as Abraham, Moses, John, and others, عَلَيْهِمُ ٱلسَّلَامُ.

Such a prohibition appears to me next to impossible, and so if that were permissible, then the tombs of the friends [of God], the scholars, and the saints must also be included [in the permission]. Just as visiting [those saints and scholars] during their lives may be a goal and a legitimate reason to travel, it is possible that visiting

---

66 Al-Tirmidhī, *Sunan*, 3917; Ibn Mājah, *Sunan*, 3112.

67 Al-Bukhārī, *Ṣaḥīḥ*, 2038; Muslim, *Ṣaḥīḥ*, 2174. In his commentary, al-Zabīdī explains that the meaning here is "Do not travel to a mosque, except to pray in these three mosques." Al-Zabīdī, *Itḥāf*, 4:286.

68 Muslim, *Ṣaḥīḥ*, 4:89.

[the sites of their graves] may be as well. This [all concerns the question of] travel.

As for residence, if the purpose of a disciple's journey is not to acquire knowledge, then it is best for him to remain where he is as long as his condition in that place is beneficial for him. If [it is] not, then he must seek a place where it is easier to live in obscurity, where his *dīn* is safer, his heart [is] free [of worries], and his worship [is] easier to accomplish. That is the best place for [a disciple]. [And as] the Prophet ﷺ said, "All lands are God's lands and all creatures are His worshipers. Wherever you find kindness, there you should live, and give praise and thanks to God تَعَالَىٰ."[69]

And it has been conveyed in a tradition, "Whoever finds his provision in something, he should stay with it, and whoever's subsistence has been placed in some particular thing, he should not leave it unless it is changed for him."[70]

Abu Nuʿaym said, "I saw Sufyān al-Thawrī put his bag on his shoulder and pick up his sandals and I asked him, 'Where [are you heading] O Abū ʿAbdallāh?' He said, 'To a land where I may fill this bag with dirhams.'"

> In another account, [Sufyān] said, "I have been told that there is a village where [living] is inexpensive, so I [could afford to] live there."
>
> [Abū Nuʿaym] said, "You would do that, O Abū ʿAbdallāh?"
>
> And he [Sufyān] replied, "Yes. If you hear of a town that is inexpensive, head to it. You will be safer in your *dīn* and have fewer concerns."[71]

He would also say, "This is an evil time. If even those who live in obscurity are not safe, what about those who become well-known? This is a time of travel when a man must go from town to town, fleeing with [his] *dīn* from tribulation (*fitan*)."[72]

---

69 Ibn Ḥanbal, *Musnad*, 1:166, with similar wording.

70 Ibn Mājah, *Sunan*, 2147, with similar wording.

71 Abū Ṭālib al-Makkī, *Qūt al-qulūb*, 2:123. The Abū Nuʿaym mentioned here is al-Faḍl b. Dukayn. Both these narrations mean that a person should try to live where he has fewer worries about earning a living, so as to be able to devote more time to worship and the remembrance of God.

72 Abū Ṭālib al-Makkī, *Qūt al-qulūb*, 2:123.

It is also recounted that [Sufyān] said,

"By God, I do not know which land to live in."

Some people said, "Khurāsān?"

He [Sufyān] said, "[There are] diverse doctrines and corrupt opinions [there]!"

Someone said, "[greater] Syria?"

He [Sufyān] answered, "People point at you there with their fingers," by which he meant you become well-known.

Then someone said, "Iraq?"

He [Sufyān] said, "That is a land of tyrants."

Another said, "Mecca?"

He [Sufyān] said, "Mecca melts your body and your purse."[73]

A stranger said to him, "I have resolved to take up residence in Mecca, so please give me counsel."

He [Sufyān] said, "I counsel you concerning three things. Do not pray in the first row, do not keep company with a Qurayshī, and do not make a show of your charity."[74]

[Sufyān] disliked the first row because it makes a person well-known, such that if he is absent, people notice his absence, and this leads to ostentation and affectation.

Section 2: On the Conditions for the Validity of the Pilgrimage, Its Pillars, Obligations, and Prohibitions

On the conditions [for the validity] of the pilgrimage

THERE are two conditions that determine the validity of pilgrimage: [to complete it in] its time and [to be a] Muslim.

73 Abū Ṭālib al-Makkī, *Qūt al-qulūb*, 2:122. Al-Zabīdī explains that "melting your purse" refers to the cost of living, which was very high there, because food was all imported. By "melting your body" he means the effort you must make to live up to the honor and sanctity of the place. Al-Zabīdī, *Itḥāf*, 4:287.

74 Abū Ṭālib al-Makkī, *Qūt al-qulūb*, 2:122.

The pilgrimage of a child is valid. If he has reached the age of discernment, he may enter *iḥrām* by himself,[75] but if he is still very young, his parent or guardian must enter it for him, accompany him on all the rites of the pilgrimage, such as the *ṭawāf*, the course (*saʿī*) [between Ṣafā and Marwā], and the rest.

The time for pilgrimage is Shawwāl and Dhū l-Qaʿda, and [from] the ninth of Dhū l-Ḥijja to the dawn of the day of sacrifice (*yawm al-naḥr*). Whoever enters *iḥrām* for the pilgrimage at any time other than this period is performing the visit (*ʿumra*) instead.

For the visit, the entire year is a valid time, but whoever dedicates himself to the rites performed during the days of Minā should not enter *iḥrām* for the visit, for he will not be able to complete it immediately after [those rites are performed] since he will [still] be taken up with the rites of Minā.

There are five criteria [for the validity of] the pilgrimage of Islam (*ḥajjat al-islām*):[76] Islam, freedom, maturity, reason, and its time.[77]

If a minor or a slave enters *iḥrām*, then the slave [must be] free or the minor [must reach] maturity while at Mount ʿArafa or at Muzdalifa, and return to ʿArafa before dawn, then he would be considered as having completed the obligatory pilgrimage of Islam. This is because "the pilgrimage is ʿArafa,"[78] and no sacrifice or expiation would be required of them other than the sheep [on the day of the sacrifice].

---

75 The verb *yuḥrimu*, translated above as "enter *iḥrām*," includes bathing and donning the pilgrim's garb at the proper station and resolving to avoid certain things, as explained on p. 36. Because of the complexity of all that is included in this term, we have transliterated the Arabic word.

76 Al-Ghazālī calls the obligatory pilgrimage *ḥajjat al-islām* (the "pilgrimage of Islam") in reference to the famous *ḥadīth* of Gabriel, which recounts the Prophet Muḥammad's ﷺ answer to Gabriel's question, "And tell me (O Muḥammad), what is Islam," the Prophet ﷺ enumerated the five pillars, the fifth of which is "that you complete the pilgrimage to the sacred house if you are able." This pilgrimage is obligatory on a Muslim at least once in his or her lifetime, if he or she is able.

77 That is, one must be Muslim; be free, i.e., not a slave; have reached maturity; be of sound mind; and it must be performed in the pilgrimage season.

78 Here he is quoting the well-known *ḥadīth* in al-Tirmidhī, *Sunan*, 889; al-Nasāʾī, *Sunan*, 3016. ʿArafa is 22 km (14 miles) from Mecca; Muzdalifa is 9 km (6 miles) from ʿArafa; Minā is 6 km (4 miles) from Muzdalifa, and Mecca is 8 km (5 miles) from Minā.

With the exception of time, these are the conditions which also apply to [a minor or a slave] completing the visit (ʿ*umra*) instead of the obligatory pilgrimage.

The conditions for the completion of a supererogatory pilgrimage on behalf of a free adult

THE person must have already completed the pilgrimage of Islam, because the obligatory takes precedence over the supererogatory. [Next,] he can make up an invalid pilgrimage if he was a slave [when he first performed the rites, and then was freed]. After that, he can perform the pilgrimage in fulfillment of a vow (*nadhr*), then on behalf of someone else (*niyāba*), and finally, a supererogatory (*nafl*) [pilgrimage]. This is the required order and this is how it is counted even if [the pilgrim] intended otherwise.[79]

There are five conditions on which the pilgrimage becomes obligatory on a person: Islam [i.e., he/she is Muslim], [has reached] maturity, [is of] sound mind, [is] free, and [is] able.

And for whomever the pilgrimage is obligatory, the visit is [also] obligatory.[80] Also, according to one view, if someone intends to enter Mecca for the purpose of an ordinary visit or for commerce—other than those employed to clear away brush—then it is incumbent on him to enter *iḥrām* and it is lawful to perform both the pilgrimage and the visit.

As for ability, this may be one of two sorts.

The first sort is [called] "immediate" ability, and it relates to several factors.

It concerns [the pilgrim] himself; in this case, it means physical health.

It concerns the road, and whether it passes through regions that are fertile and safe, [is] free of [the need] to cross dangerous waters, or [encounter] powerful enemies.

It may also concern wealth. A person must have enough to pay for travel [to Mecca] and return to his homeland, regardless of

79 For example, if he expressed the intention to complete the pilgrimage in fulfillment of a vow or for someone else, but had not yet completed his own obligatory pilgrimage, then the rites would be counted as in fulfillment of the obligatory pilgrimage.

80 Al-Ghazālī is referring to the point of view of some scholars, that the visit (ʿ*umra*) is also an obligatory (*farḍ*) act of worship.

whether he has a family or not, for to leave one's homeland is always hard. [In the case of dependents], he must have enough to provide for them in his absence, and enough to settle any debts that are due. He must be able to afford to buy a riding camel or at least to rent one along with a litter, or at the very least [rent] a pack animal.[81]

The second sort of ability is that of someone whose health is frail, but who has enough wealth to pay for someone to perform a pilgrimage on his behalf, provided the hired person has already completed the pilgrimage of Islam for himself. In this case, it is sufficient for [the sick person] to be able to pay for a pack animal.

Thus, if a son offers [to complete the pilgrimage] for a frail parent, then that parent is considered able. But if the son only offers his [frail] parent the money needed to make the trip, the parent, by that fact alone, is not considered able. In physical service there is honor for the son and in giving money there is benevolence toward the parent.

Thus, the pilgrimage becomes obligatory on whoever has the ability. Someone may delay going, but there is a danger in doing so. If he is accorded the chance to go, even in the latter part of his life, the obligation should be fulfilled, but if he dies before having completed the pilgrimage, he meets God as one who has disobeyed [one of God's commandments] by omitting it. That pilgrimage then becomes part of his legacy, to be performed on his behalf [by someone else], whether this is mentioned in his will or not, for it is considered a debt like other debts.[82] However, if someone had been able [to perform the pilgrimage] one year but failed to set out with the people and then, subsequently, lost his wealth before the [next time] people were departing for the pilgrimage, and then he died, he would meet God عَزَّوَجَلَّ without the pilgrimage due on him.

Whoever dies without having completed the pilgrimage, but with the means to do so, is in a precarious state before God عَزَّوَجَلَّ. Thus ʿUmar رَضِيَ ٱللَّهُ عَنْهُ said, "I considered imposing a tax on those in

81 Here al-Ghazālī is addressing the question of traveling to Mecca on foot. According to one view, if someone is unable to afford a mount, then distance and strength permitting, they are obliged to go on foot, with only a pack animal to carry their supplies.

82 In several places, the Qurʾān repeats that the inheritance goes to the family only *after any bequest he [may have] made or debt* [4:11 and 4:12].

the frontier provinces who are able to perform the pilgrimage, but do not."[83]

Saʿīd b. Jubayr, Ibrāhīm al-Nakhaʿī, Mujāhid, and Ṭāwūs each said, "If I knew of a rich man on whom the pilgrimage was obligatory but who died without performing it, I would not offer the [funeral] prayer for him."[84]

One of them, in fact, had a wealthy neighbor who died without ever performing the pilgrimage, and [he] did not offer the [funeral] prayer for him [the neighbor].[85]

Ibn ʿAbbās said, "One who dies without paying *zakāt* or performing the pilgrimage will be among those who ask to be returned to this world," and then he recited the verse,

حَتَّىٰٓ إِذَا جَآءَ أَحَدَهُمُ ٱلْمَوْتُ قَالَ رَبِّ ٱرْجِعُونِ ﴿٩٩﴾ لَعَلِّيٓ أَعْمَلُ صَٰلِحًا فِيمَا تَرَكْتُ

[*For such is the state of the disbelievers*], *until, when death comes to one of them, he says, "My Lord, send me back that I might do righteousness in that which I left behind"* [23:99–100].

Ibn ʿAbbās added, "[This refers to] the pilgrimage."[86]

The five pillars [required] for a valid pilgrimage

[THESE five pillars are] to enter *iḥrām*, to perform *ṭawāf*, to follow this with the course (*saʿī*), to stand at ʿArafa, and, according to one opinion, to follow that by cutting one's hair.[87] These are also the pillars of the visit, with the exception of standing at ʿArafa.

There are six obligatory elements which, if omitted, must be amended with the blood of a sacrifice.[88] The first of these is to enter

83 Al-Lālakāʾī, *Iʿtiqād ahl al-sunna*, 2:924.

84 Ibn Abī Shayba, *al-Muṣannaf*, 14668 and 14666. This is also recounted in Abū Ṭālib al-Makkī, *Qūt al-qulūb*, 2:114.

85 Abū Ṭālib al-Makkī, *Qūt al-qulūb*, 2:114.

86 Al-Tirmidhī, *Sunan*, 3316.

87 According to another opinion, shaving the head is among the obligatory elements (*wājibāt*) mentioned next.

88 All of the meat of this sacrifice, be it lamb, beef, or camel, must be given to the poor.

iḥrām at one of the stations (*mīqāt*). If someone misses doing this and then goes past the station without *iḥrām*, he must sacrifice a sheep as expiation. The second is throwing the pebbles.[89] According to the unanimous opinion of the learned, if this is omitted, it must be rectified with a sacrifice. As for remaining at ʿArafa until sunset, camping at Muzdalifa, camping at Minā, and the farewell *ṭawāf*, if any of these [four] are omitted, according to one of two opinions, they must be expiated with a sacrifice. The other opinion holds that a sacrifice in their case is [not obligatory] but recommended.

The pilgrimage may be combined with the visit in three ways.

The first way is called "individual" (*ifrād*), and is the most meritorious. This means completing the pilgrimage by itself and then going somewhere outside the sacred precinct (*ḥill*) to enter into *iḥrām* anew and then complete the rites of the visit. The best place outside the sacred precinct to re-enter *iḥrām* for the visit is Jiʿrāna, then Tanʿīm, and [third in merit is] al-Ḥudaybiyya.[90] No sacrifice is needed by someone who chooses to complete the individual visit, although it [a sacrifice] may be done as a supererogatory act.

The second way is called "joined" (*qirān*). This means that the pilgrim combines [the rites of both]. He says, "Here I am, O Lord, for both pilgrimage and visit" and thereby enters *iḥrām* for both. Thereafter, to complete the rites for the pilgrimage suffices, since [the rites] of the visit are included, just as the lesser ablution (*wuḍūʾ*) is included in the greater ablution (*ghusl*).[91] However, if he completes the *ṭawāf* and the course (*saʿī*) before standing at ʿArafa, the course counts for both rites, but the circumambulation does not count because it is a condition of the obligatory *ṭawāf* of the pilgrimage that it must follow ʿArafa. This means that sacrificing a sheep is [always] required of the one who chooses this method of performing both the pilgrimage and the visit, unless he is a resident of Mecca, in which case nothing is required of him because he has not left his station (*mīqāt*) of entering *iḥrām*, which is Mecca.

---

89 This refers to the symbolic stoning of the devil that takes place at Minā.

90 Jiʿrāna is about twelve miles from Mecca on the road to Taif. Tanʿīm, the closest, is a little more than four miles from Mecca, and al-Ḥudaybiyya, famous for the treaty that was signed there, is approximately nine miles from Mecca.

91 See Book 3 of the *Revival of the Religous Sciences: The Mysteries of Purification*, for the lesser ablution (*wuḍūʾ*), 27–34; and for the greater ablution (*ghusl*), 36–37.

The third way is called "enjoyment" (*tamattuʿ*).[92] This means that the pilgrim leaves his station in *iḥrām* for the visit, [completes that], leaves *iḥrām* in Mecca, and enjoys what was prohibited to him [while he was in *iḥrām*]. Then, when the time for the rites of the pilgrimage arrives, he re-enters *iḥrām* for it. For someone to be considered *mutamattiʿ*,[93] there are five conditions.

First, he must not be among those who reside near the sacred mosque, and this means those who live so close that they are not permitted to shorten their prayers as travelers.

Second, he must perform the visit before the pilgrimage.

Third, he must perform the visit during the months of the pilgrimage.

Fourth, he must not return to the station [where he entered *iḥrām* for the visit], or go a similar distance, in order to re-enter *iḥrām* for the pilgrimage.

Fifth, both the pilgrimage and the visit must be done for one and the same person.

If these conditions are realized, he is *mutamattiʿ* and it is necessary for him to offer a sheep as sacrifice. If he cannot do that, he must fast for three days, consecutively or separately, during the time of the pilgrimage [but] before the day of sacrifice (*yawm al-naḥr*), and then seven [additional days] when he returns to his homeland. If he does not fast the three days [in Mecca] then he must fast ten [days] at home, either consecutively or separately. Fasting in place of sacrificing a sheep is the same in the case of the joined visit and pilgrimage (*qirān*) or the pilgrimage preceded by the visit (*tamattuʿ*).

[In terms of which method of completing the pilgrimage and visit is preferred], *ifrād* is considered best, then *tamattuʿ*, and lastly *qirān*.

The six actions that are prohibited during the pilgrimage and visit

The first is wearing shirts, pantaloons, leather foot coverings, or turbans. Rather, the pilgrim should wear a simple [unsewn] cloth around [his] loins (*īzār*), an upper cloth (*ridāʾ*) over [his] shoulders,

---

92 This term is used because the visit is completed first and the pilgrim leaves the state of *iḥrām*. This permits the enjoyments that are forbidden while in *iḥrām*, discussed below, before re-entering that state in order to complete the pilgrimage.

93 Someone following this way of completing the visit and pilgrimage together.

and sandals. If he does not have sandals, then it is permissible to wear leather foot coverings, provided they been cut so that the ankles are bare. Also, if he does not have a lower cloth, then wide pantaloons are allowed. There is also no harm [in wearing] a waistband and taking shade from something carried,[94] but [a male pilgrim] may not wear anything normally designated as a head covering[95] since his [bare head] is [part of] *iḥrām* [for him].

A woman may wear any sewn garment but she must not cover her face with anything that touches it since her [bare] face is [part of] *iḥrām* [for her].

The second prohibition is perfume. [The pilgrim] should avoid using anything that reasonable people would consider a scent. If he does [use perfume], or wears [any clothing that is prohibited], he must sacrifice a sheep [as expiation].

The third prohibition is cutting the hair and trimming [the nails]. Expiation for this is sacrificing a sheep. However, there is no harm in [using] kohl, entering the [public] bathhouse, bloodletting, cupping, or combing the hair.

The fourth prohibition is sexual intercourse. If this takes place before the first stage of leaving *iḥrām*,[96] then the pilgrimage is invalidated and a person is required [to sacrifice] a camel, a cow, or seven sheep as expiation. However, if it occurs after the first stage, the pilgrimage remains valid, but it is still obligatory to sacrifice a camel.

The fifth prohibition is [encouraging] those activities that can lead to sexual intercourse, such as kissing and embracing, both of which break the ablution if done [between] a woman and a man. These are prohibited and, like masturbation, require the sacrifice of a sheep as expiation. To marry and to contract a marriage are also forbidden, but there is no sacrifice if they are done, because [the marriage is not valid].

---

94 Generally, this is an umbrella, but could be something like a bag in which belongings are carried.

95 Meaning any sort of cap or hat.

96 There are two stages to leaving the state of *iḥrām*. The first occurs when the pilgrim has completed any two of the final three rites: casting the stones, cutting the hair, and *ṭawāf* following ʿArafa (*al-ṭawāf al-ifāḍa*). After doing any two of these, the first stage of leaving *iḥrām* is complete and all things apart from sexual intercourse, contracting marriage, or sexual contact are permissible.

The sixth prohibition is the killing of wild game, meaning whatever is, in itself, lawful to eat or is born from the mating of a lawful and a prohibited animal. If the pilgrim kills game, he must sacrifice whatever domestic livestock most resembles the animal killed, in view of the resemblance between the species. Fishing, however, is lawful and there is no penalty for it.

2

On the Order of the Outward Actions from the Beginning of the Journey Until the Return

This chapter is in ten parts

Part 1: The Eight [Actions] Which Must Be Observed from the Initial Departure to the *Iḥrām*

THE **first** concerns money. [Someone intending to set out on the pilgrimage] needs to begin with repentance, and this includes redressing any wrongs he has committed against others and repaying debts. He should also have enough money in hand to provide for those who are dependent on him, return anything given to him for safekeeping, and take with him on the journey only money that has been acquired in a pure and lawful way. This should be enough to travel there and back without being stingy. On the contrary, it should be enough so that a pilgrim can be generous with his provision and charitable toward the weak and the needy. In fact, he should give charity before he sets out, and purchase or rent for himself an animal strong enough to bear his load and not become weak. If he rents the animal, he must show the one who is renting it to him everything that he intends to load on it, great or small, so that the renter [the one renting the animal to him] is satisfied with the arrangement.[1]

1 "Even if this means giving him something in addition to the agreed price in order to ensure that he is satisfied and any doubtful aspects of the arrangement are

The **second** concerns the traveling companion. [The pilgrim] should find a companion who is pious, who loves goodness, and wants to complete it [the pilgrimage]. If the pilgrim forgets, his companion will remind him;[2] if he remembers, his companion will help him; if he grows fearful, his companion will encourage him; if he cannot do something, his companion will strengthen him; if he becomes frustrated, his companion will help him to be patient.

As for the loved ones who remain behind, [including] his brethren, and his neighbors, he should bid them farewell and ask for their supplications, for God تَعَالَىٰ will bless their supplications. The *sunna* of farewell is to say,

أستودع الله دينك، وأمانتك، وخواتيم عملك

> I commit to God's safekeeping your *dīn*, all that is entrusted to you, and the deeds with which [your stay] is ended.[3]

And the Prophet صَلَّىٱللَّهُعَلَيْهِوَسَلَّمَ used to say to anyone who was setting out on a journey,

في حفظ الله وكنفه، زودك الله التقوى، وغفر ذنبك، ووجهك للخير أينما كنت

> May you remain in God's protection and shelter, and may God increase your piety, forgive your sins, and direct you to goodness wherever you may be.[4]

The **third** concerns leaving one's home. When the pilgrim has resolved to leave his home, he should pray two cycles.[5] In the first, after [Sūrat al-] Fātiḥa, he should recite *Say, O disbelievers* [Sūrat 109], and in the second, al-Ikhlāṣ [Sūrat 112]. When he completes the prayer, [he should] raise his hands in supplication and call on God, سُبۡحَانَهُ, with pure sincerity and true intentions.

---

removed." Al-Zabīdī, *Itḥāf*, 4:324.

2 That is, if he forgets to complete something that is part of the goodness of the pilgrimage, his companion will remind him of it.

3 Abū Dāwūd, *Sunan*, 2600; Ibn Mājah, *Sunan*, 2826.

4 Al-Dārimī, *Sunan*, 271; al-Tirmidhī, *Sunan*, 3444, but without the first phrase.

5 Throughout the translation, we use the word "cycle" to translate *rakʿa*, meaning a complete cycle of the prayer including standing, bowing (*rukūʿ*), and prostrating.

اللّٰهُمَّ، أَنتَ الصّاحِبُ في السَّفرِ، والـخَليفَةُ في الأَهلِ والـمالِ والولد والأصحاب، احفظنا وإياهم من كل آفة وعاهة، اللّٰهُمَّ، إنا نسألك في مسيرنا هذا البر والتقوى ومن العمل ما ترضى، اللّٰهُمَّ، إنا نسألك أن تطوي لنا الأرض ،وتهون علينا السفر، وأن ترزقنا في سفرنا سلامة البدن والدين والمال، وتبلغنا حج بيتك، وزيارة قبر نبيك محمد صَلَّى ٱللَّهُ عَلَيْهِ وَسَلَّمَ، اللّٰهُمَّ، إنا نعوذ بك من وعثاء السفر، وكآبة المنظر، وسوء المنقلب في الأهل والمال والولد والأصحاب، اللّٰهُمَّ، اجعلنا وإياهم في جوارك، ولا تسلبنا وإياهم نعمتك، ولا تغير ما بنا وبهم من عافيتك

O God! You are the companion in the journey and You are the one I leave behind to watch over my family, wealth, children, and friends. Protect us and them from all calamities and illness. O God, we ask You for goodness and piety in our journey, and [to make our] deeds pleasing to You. O God, shorten for us the earth over which we travel, make our journey easy, provide for us in our journey with safety in our bodies, our *dīn*, and our possessions. Allow us to complete the pilgrimage to Your house and to visit the tomb of Your Prophet, Muḥammad صَلَّى ٱللَّهُ عَلَيْهِ وَسَلَّمَ. O God, we take refuge in You from the weariness of travel, from sadness on return, or from the sight of any harm to our families, possessions, children, and friends. O God, keep us and them near You, do not deprive us or them of Your grace, and do not take from us or them the well-being You have granted.[6]

The **fourth** [concerns] when [the pilgrim] reaches the door of his home. There, he should say,

بسم الله، توكلت على الله، ولا حول ولا قوة إلا بالله، أعوذ بالله، رب أعوذ بك أن أضل، أو أضل، أو أذل، أو أذل، أو أزل، أو أزل، أو أظلم، أو أظلم، أو أجهل، أو يجهل علي، اللّٰهُمَّ، إني لم أخرج أشرا ولا بطرا، ولا رياء ولا سمعة، بل خرجت اتقاء سخطك، وابتغاء مرضاتك، وقضاء فرضك، واتباع سنة نبيك، وشوقا إلى لقائك

In the name of God, I put my trust in God, there is no strength nor power but in God! O Lord, I take refuge in You from

6 This includes much of the supplication for setting out on a journey that is included in Muslim, *Ṣaḥīḥ*, 1342, and elsewhere.

> leading another astray or being led astray, from humiliating another or being humiliated, from making another slip or being made to slip, from wronging another or being wronged, from keeping another ignorant of something or being kept ignorant. O God, I go forth neither arrogantly nor boastfully, and not so people may see me or may talk about me. Rather, I go forth mindful of Your anger, seeking Your good pleasure, fulfilling what You have enjoined, following the *sunna* of Your Prophet, and yearning for the meeting with You.

Then, as he starts walking, he should say,

> اللّٰهُمَّ، بك انتشرت، وعليك توكلت، وبك اعتصمت، وإليك توجهت، اللّٰهُمَّ، أنت ثقتي، وأنت رجائي، فاكفني ما أهمني، وما لا أهتم به، وما أنت أعلم به مني، عز جارك، وجل ثناؤك، ولا إلٰه غيرك، اللّٰهُمَّ، زودني التقوى، واغفر لي ذنبي، ووجهني للخير أينما توجهت
>
> O God! By You I set out, and on you I place my trust, and in You I seek shelter, and toward You I turn. O God, You are my trust and You are my hope. Suffice me in the things that worry me and the things that do not, and You know better than I what they are. Fortify [those who] seek Your shelter and how great is Your praise! There is no god but You. O God, [for the journey] provide for me with piety, forgive me my sins, and wherever I turn [my] face, turn it toward goodness.

He should say this prayer when departing from each stop along the way.

The **fifth** [concerns] riding [his animal]. When he is about to ride [it], [the pilgrim should] say,

> بسم الله، وبالله، والله أكبر ،توكلت على الله، ولا حول ولا قوة إلا بالله العلي العظيم، ما شاء الله كان، وما لم يشأ لم يكن
>
> In the name of God, and by God, and God is greater! I place my trust in God. There is no strength nor power except in God, the most high, the mighty. Whatever God wills, happens, and whatever He does not will, does not happen.

لِتَسْتَوُۥا۟ عَلَىٰ ظُهُورِهِۦ ثُمَّ تَذْكُرُوا۟ نِعْمَةَ رَبِّكُمْ إِذَا ٱسْتَوَيْتُمْ عَلَيْهِ وَتَقُولُوا۟
سُبْحَـٰنَ ٱلَّذِى سَخَّرَ لَنَا هَـٰذَا وَمَا كُنَّا لَهُۥ مُقْرِنِينَ ﴿١٣﴾ وَإِنَّآ إِلَىٰ رَبِّنَا لَمُنقَلِبُونَ ﴿١٤﴾

That you may settle yourselves on their backs and then remember the favor of your Lord when you have settled on them and say. "Exalted is He who has subjected this to us, and we could not have [otherwise] subdued it. And indeed we, to our Lord, will [surely] return" [43:13–14].

اللّٰهُمَّ، إني وجهت وجهي إليك، وفوضت أمري كله إليك، وتوكلت في جميع أموري عليك، أنت حسبي ونعم الوكيل

> O God, I turn my face toward You, I place this journey in Your hands, I place my trust in You in all things. You are sufficient for me and the best in whom to put my trust.

And when he is seated on his mount and it is standing still beneath him, he should say,

سبحان الله والحمد لله ولا إله إلا الله والله أكبر سبع مرات

> Glory be to God, Praise be to God, there is no god except God, and God is most great,

seven times. Then he should say,

وَقَالُوا۟ ٱلْحَمْدُ لِلَّهِ ٱلَّذِى هَدَىٰنَا لِهَـٰذَا وَمَا كُنَّا لِنَهْتَدِىَ لَوْلَآ أَنْ هَدَىٰنَا ٱللَّهُ

Praise to God, who has guided us to this; and we would never have been guided if God had not guided us [7:43].

الله اللّٰهُمَّ أنت الحامل على الظهر وأنت المستعان على الأمور

> O God, You are the One who bears me on this [camel's] back, and You are the One who helps me in all matters.

The **sixth** concerns resting during the journey. The *sunna* here is not to stop until the day heats up so the greater part of the journey is at night, even as the Prophet ﷺ said, "I enjoin on you journeying by night, for the [distances over the] earth are folded up at night in a way that they are not during the day."[7]

[The pilgrim] should sleep little at night, as it will help in his journey and whenever he comes in view of a stopping [place], he should say,

> اللّٰهُمَّ رب السموات السبع وما أظللن، ورب الأرضين السبع وما أقللن، ورب الشياطين وما أضللن، ورب الرياح وما ذرين، ورب البحار وما جرين، أسألك خير هذا المنزل، وخير أهله، وأعوذ بك من شره وشر ما فيه، اصرف عني شر شرارهم
>
> O God! Lord of the seven skies and what they shade, Lord of the seven earths and what they bear, Lord of the devils and those whom they lead astray, Lord of the winds and what they disperse, Lord of the seas and what they carry off! I ask You for the good of this place and the good of those who inhabit it, and I seek refuge in You from the evil of this place, from the evil of those who inhabit it, and from the evil of what it contains. Turn away from me the evil of the worst of them.

Then, when he gets off [his mount] to rest in that place, he should pray two cycles then say,

> أعوذ بكلمات الله التامات التي لا يجاوزهن بر ولا فاجر من شر ما خلق
>
> I seek refuge in the totality of God's words, which neither a good man nor a sinful one may trespass, from the evil of anything which God created.

And when the night falls, he should say,

> يا أرضُ، ربِّي وربُّكِ اللهُ، أعوذُ باللهِ مِنْ شرِّكِ وشرِّ ما فيكِ، وشرِّ ما دبَّ عليكِ، أعوذُ باللهِ مِنْ شرِّ كلِّ أسدٍ وأسودَ، وحيَّةٍ وعقربٍ، ومِنْ شرِّ ساكنِ البلدِ، ووالدٍ وما ولدَ،
>
> O earth! My Lord and your Lord is God. I seek refuge in God from your evil, the evil of what is in you, and the evil of what moves across you. I seek refuge in God from the evil of every lion, serpent, snake, and scorpion, and from the evil of any who might live in this land and the parent and what he begat.

---

7 Abū Dāwūd, *Sunan*, 2571, but without the phrase, "in a way they are not during the day."

۞وَلَهُۥ مَا سَكَنَ فِي ٱلَّيۡلِ وَٱلنَّهَارِۚ وَهُوَ ٱلسَّمِيعُ ٱلۡعَلِيمُ ﴿١٣﴾

And to Him belongs that which reposes by night and by day, and He is the Hearing, the Knowing [6:13].

The **seventh** concerns being on guard. [The pilgrim] should be cautious during the day. He should not walk off by himself away from the caravan, lest he be slain [by malefactors or beasts] or lose his way. [He should also] be on his guard at night [especially] while sleeping. If he sleeps in the beginning of the night, he may spread out his arms, but if he sleeps in the later part of the night, then he should fold one arm up such that his head lies on his palm. This was how the Messenger ﷺ of God slept while traveling.[8] Otherwise, his sleep might become so heavy that the sun will rise without his knowledge and [it may be] that the [obligatory] prayer he missed was better for him than all he could gain from the pilgrimage.

It is most desirable for the two traveling companions to take turns standing guard at night: while one sleeps, the other guards. This is the *sunna*. If an enemy or predatory animal heads in his direction, by night or day, he should recite the verse of the throne [2:255],[9] the verse *God witnesses that there is no deity except Him* [3:18],[10] then Sūrat al-Ikhlāṣ [112] and the two *sūras* of seeking refuge [113 and 114]. Then he should say,

8 As is recounted in Muslim, *Ṣaḥīḥ*, 683.

9 The meaning of the verse of the throne is as follows: *God—there is no deity except Him, the Ever-Living, the Sustainer of* [*all*] *existence. Neither drowsiness overtakes Him nor sleep. To Him belongs whatever is in the heavens and whatever is on the earth. Who is it that can intercede with Him except by His permission? He knows what is* [*presently*] *before them and what will be after them, and they encompass not a thing of His knowledge except for what He wills. His throne extends over the heavens and the earth, and their preservation tires Him not. And He is the Most High, the Most Great* [2:255].

10 Al-Ghazālī is referring to these words: *God witnesses that there is no deity except Him, and* [*so do*] *the angels and those of knowledge—*[*that He is*] *maintaining* [*creation*] *in justice. There is no god except Him, the exalted in might, the wise. Indeed, the dīn in the sight of God is Islam* [3:18–19].

بسمِ اللهِ ما شاءَ اللهُ، لا قوةَ إلا باللهِ، حسبيَ اللهُ، توكَّلتُ على اللهِ، ما شاءَ اللهُ لا يأتي بالخيرِ إلا اللهُ، ما شاءُ اللهُ لا يصرفُ السوءَ إلا اللهُ، حسبيَ اللهُ وكفى، سمعَ اللهُ لمنْ دعا، ليسَ وراءَ الله منتهىً، ولا دونَ اللهِ ملجأ،

In the name of God. Whatever God wills, there is no strength except in God, God is sufficient for me, and I place my trust in God. Whatever God wills, no one brings goodness except God. Whatever God wills, no one turns away bad except God. God suffices me. God hears the one who calls to Him. There is no limit beyond God and no refuge other than God.

كَتَبَ ٱللَّهُ لَأَغْلِبَنَّ أَنَا۠ وَرُسُلِىٓۚ إِنَّ ٱللَّهَ قَوِىٌّ عَزِيزٌ ﴿٢١﴾

God has written, "I will surely overcome, I and My messengers." Indeed, God is Powerful and Exalted in Might [58:21].

تحصنتُ باللهِ العظيمِ، واستغثتُ بالحيِّ الذي لا يموتُ، اللّٰهُمَّ، احرسنا بعينِكَ التي لا تنامُ، واكنفْنا بركْنِكَ الذي لا يُرامُ، اللّٰهُمَّ، ارحمْنا بقدرتِكَ علينا، فلا نهلَكُ وأنت ثقتُنا ورجاؤُنا، اللّٰهُمَّ ،اعطفْ علينا قلوبَ عبادِكَ وإمائِكَ برأفةٍ ورحمةٍ إنَّكَ أنتَ أرحمُ الراحمينَ.

I am strengthened and protected in almighty God, and I seek help from the Eternally Living, the One who does not die. O God, watch over us with Your eye that does not sleep, and shelter me with Your support that will not be moved. O God, be merciful to us through Your power over us, and let us not perish while You are our trust and our hope. O God, let the hearts of Your servants, men and women, incline toward us with compassion and mercy. Verily, You are the Most Merciful of the merciful.

The **eighth** concerns ascending a grade along the way. [When doing this] it is recommended that he repeat the formula of magnification [*Allāhu akbar*: God is great] three times, and say,

اللّٰهُمَّ، لكَ الشرفُ على كلِّ شرفٍ، ولكَ الحمدُ على كلِّ حالٍ

O God, Your elevation (*sharaf*)[11] is above all others, and Yours is the praise in every state.

Then, when he has reached the crest and descends, he should pronounce the formula of glorification [*subḥān Allāh*: glory be to God]. And whenever he fears loneliness in his travel, he [should] say,

سبحانَ الله الملكِ القدوسِ، ربِّ الملائكةِ والروحِ، جلَّلتَ السمواتِ بالعزَّةِ والجبروتِ

glory be to God, the King, the Venerated One, the Lord of angels and the spirit—You have clothed the heavens in honor and might.[12]

Part 2: The Five Actions Which Must Be Observed on Entering *Iḥrām* from the Station until the Entrance to Mecca

FIRST, the pilgrim must take a complete bath and do so with the intention of completing the greater ablution (*ghusl*) for the sake of entering *iḥrām*. When he reaches the well-known station (*mīqāt*) where the people [coming from his land] enter *iḥrām*, he should complete his greater ablution by cleaning [himself], then combing his hair and beard, trimming his nails, cutting his moustache, and completing the cleaning that we have mentioned in *The Book of Purification*.[13]

Second, he must rid himself of all sewn clothing and don the garments of *iḥrām*, two white cloths [one worn around the loins, the other over the shoulders], for white clothing is the most beloved to God تَعَالَىٰ. Then he should apply scent to his body and clothes, and there is no harm if a trace of it remains [on the two cloths] after completing *iḥrām*, for a trace of the musk that the

11 The word *sharaf* has the meaning of something physically higher than something else, as well as nobility and honor.

12 Al-Ṭabarānī, *al-Muʿjam al-kabīr*, 2:24.

13 See Book 3 of the *Revival of the Religious Sciences: The Mysteries of Purification*.

Messenger ﷺ of God used before *iḥrām* was seen on his forehead afterward.[14]

Third, after putting on the garments [of *iḥrām*] the pilgrim should wait until his camel starts moving, if he is riding, or he himself sets out walking; if he is on foot, then, at this moment, he should express his intention to enter *iḥrām* for the sake of completing the pilgrimage or visit, either combined (*qirān*) or separately (*ifrād*), whichever he wishes.[15] The expression of intention alone is sufficient to validate *iḥrām*, but it is a *sunna* to join this expression with the words of the pilgrim's invocation (*talbiyya*):

لبيكَ اللَّهُمَّ لبيكَ، لبيكَ لا شريكَ لكَ لبيكَ، إنَّ الحمدَ والنعمةَ لكَ والمُلْكُ لا شريكَ لكَ

> Here I am at Your service, O God, here I am at Your service. There is no partner with you. Verily, for You is all praise and [from You is] all blessing, and the dominion. There is no partner with You.

If he wishes to add to this, he should say

لبيكَ وسعديكَ، والخيرُ كلُّهُ بيديكَ، والرغباءُ إليكَ، لبيكَ بحجَّةٍ حقّاً، تعبُّداً ورقّاً، اللَّهُمَّ صلِّ على محمدٍ وعلى آلِ محمدٍ

> Here I am at Your service and for Your pleasure. All goodness is through Your hands and virtue is from You. Here I am at Your service [to complete] the pilgrimage in truth, devotion, and servanthood. O God bless Muḥammad and the family of Muḥammad.[16]

Fourth, when the process of entering *iḥrām* is concluded with the *talbiyya* as mentioned, it is recommended that he say,

اللَّهُمَّ، إنِّي أريدُ الحجَّ، فيسِّرْهُ لي وأعنِّي على أداءِ فرضِهِ وتقبَّلْهُ منِّي، اللَّهُمَّ، إنِّي نويتُ أداءَ فريضتِكَ في الحجِّ، فاجعلني من الذين استجابوا لك وآمنوا بوعدك واتبعوا أمرك،

---

14 Al-Bukhārī, *Ṣaḥīḥ*, 271; Muslim, *Ṣaḥīḥ*, 1190.

15 In *al-Wajīz*, al-Ghazālī adds that a prayer of two cycles should also be offered at this time. See al-Rāfiʿī, *al-ʿAzīz*, 3:380.

16 Al-Bukhārī, *Ṣaḥīḥ*, 1549; Muslim, *Ṣaḥīḥ*, 1184.

> واجعلني مِنْ وفدِكَ الذينَ رضيتَ عنهُمْ وارتضيتَ وقبلْتَ منهُمْ، اللّٰهُمَّ، فيسَّرْ لي أداءَ ما نويتُ مِنَ الحجَّ، اللّٰهُمَّ، قدْ أحرمَ لكَ لحمي وشعري، ودمي وعصبي، ومخِّي وعظامي، وحرَّمْتُ على نفسي النساءَ والطيبَ ولبسَ المخيطِ ابتغاءَ وجهِكَ والدارِ الآخرةِ
>
> O God, I intend to complete the pilgrimage. [Please] make it easy for me, help me to fulfill its obligations, and accept it from me. O God, I intend to fulfill what You have enjoined in the pilgrimage, so please make me among those who have answered You, believed in Your promise, and followed Your commandment. Make me among Your visitors who are pleasing to You and from whom You accept [this worship]. O God, make it easy for me to accomplish the pilgrimage that I have intended. O God, I have sanctified to You my hair, my flesh, my blood, my nerves, my brain, and my bones. I have sanctified myself for You from women, perfume, and wearing sewn clothes—this for the sake of Your countenance and the abode of the hereafter.

From the moment of [entering] *iḥrām*, the six prohibited things previously mentioned become forbidden to him, so he should avoid them.

Fifth, it is recommended that the *talbiyya* be repeated as long as one is in *iḥrām*, especially when encountering [other] caravans, when gathering with people, when ascending or descending [hills], or when mounting or dismounting [a riding beast]. He should utter it in a raised voice, but not so loud that his voice becomes hoarse or he becomes short of breath, for it is related in a *ḥadīth*, he is not calling on someone who does not hear or someone who is absent.[17]

There is no harm in repeating the *talbiyya* aloud inside the three mosques, for they are designated as places for the rites [of the pilgrimage], and by three mosques, I mean the sacred mosque, the mosque of al-Khayf, and the mosque of the station (*mīqāt*).[18] In other mosques, there is no harm in repeating the *talbiyya*, but not

17 Al-Bukhārī, *Ṣaḥīḥ*, 2992; Muslim, *Ṣaḥīḥ*, 2704. The commentary points out that raising the voice for the *talbiyya* applies to men; women should use the same tone they use reciting aloud in the prayer. Al-Zabīdī, *Itḥāf*, 4:338.

18 Where he entered *iḥrām*.

aloud. In fact, whenever the Prophet ﷺ saw something he found marvelous, he would say

لَبَّيْكَ إِنَّ الْعَيْشَ عَيْشُ الآخِرَةِ

> Here I am at Your service! Verily, the true life is the life of the hereafter![19]

Part 3: The Six Actions Which Must Be Observed from the Entrance to Mecca up to the *Ṭawāf*

FIRST, [the pilgrim must] perform the greater ablution (*ghusl*) at Dhū Ṭuwā[20] in order to enter Mecca.

In fact, there are a total of nine stages during the pilgrimage at which it is recommended that the greater ablution be performed. First, at the station when one enters *iḥrām*, then on first entering Mecca (as mentioned here),[21] then for the standing at ʿArafa, then for the stay at Muzdalifa, and then for the stoning of the three pillars—but there is no [separate] greater ablution for the stoning the ʿAqaba pillar[22]—and last, for the farewell *ṭawāf*. However, in his revised [*madhhab*][23] al-Shafiʿī رضي الله عنه does not include the greater ablution for the *ṭawāf* on going forth from ʿArafa[24] or the farewell circumambulation, so [for him] the number is seven.

Second, on entering the beginning of the sanctuary (*ḥaram*) which is outside Mecca, [the pilgrim] should say,

19 Al-Shāfiʿī, *al-Umm*, 3:391.

20 A place near Mecca referred to the Q. 48:24 as "Baṭn Makka," or the valley of Mecca.

21 Presumably this includes the circumambulation of arrival (*ṭawāf al-qudūm*), which appears in other editions of the *Iḥyāʾ* as well as in the commentary by al-Zabīdī (*Itḥāf*, 4:340) but is not mentioned in the Dār al-Minhāj edition as a separate occasion. However, if the three pillars are considered three separate times, then the total is eight, not nine.

22 This is the third of the three pillars.

23 The early legal rulings of Imām al-Shāfiʿī رضي الله عنه (d. 204/819) from his stay in Baghdad (195–199/810–814) reflected the environment of Baghdad, and differed greatly from his later, revised (*jadīd*) legal rulings that he wrote after his move to Egypt in 199/814.

24 This is referred to as *ṭawāf al-ziyāra* in the text. The more common name, however, is *ṭawāf al-ifāḍa*.

اللّٰهُمَّ، هذا حرمُكَ وأمنُكَ، فحرِّمْ لحمي ودمي وشعري وبشري على النارِ، وآمنِّي مِنْ عذابِكَ يومَ تبعثُ عبادَكَ، واجعلني مِنْ أوليائِكَ وأهلِ طاعتِكَ

O God, this is Your sanctuary and Your safety (*āmina*), so forbid my flesh, my blood, my hair, and my body from the fire, make me safe from Your punishment on the day You bring Your servants back to life, and make me among Your friends and those who are obedient to You.

Third, the pilgrim should enter Mecca from the direction of Abṭaḥ, that is, from Kadāʾ pass.[25] [It has been related][26] that the Messenger ﷺ of God turned off the path he was on in order to so, and it is always preferable to follow his example. Then, he left the city, by the Kudā pass. That is the lower road, while Kadāʾ is the upper.[27]

Fourth, when he enters Mecca and reaches Raʾs al-Radm,[28] where his eyes catch the first glimpse of the house, he should say:

لا إله إلا اللهُ، واللهُ أكبرُ، اللّٰهُمَّ ،أنتَ السلامُ، ومنكَ السلامُ، ودارُكَ دارُ السلامِ، تباركتَ يا ذا الجلالِ والإكرامِ، اللّٰهُمَّ، إنَّ هذا بيتُكَ عظَّمْتَهُ وكرَّمْتَهُ وشرَّفْتَهُ اللّٰهُمَّ، فزِدْهُ تعظيماً وزِدْهُ تشريفاً وتكريماً، وزِدْه مهابةً، وزِدْ مَنْ حجَّهُ بِرّاً وكرامةً، اللّٰهُمَّ، افتحْ لي أبوابَ رحمتِكَ، وأدخلني جنَّتَكَ، وأعذني مِنَ الشيطانِ الرجيمِ

There is no god but God. God is most great. O God, You are peace, from You comes peace, and Your house is the house of peace. Blessed be You, endowed with majesty and generosity. O God! This is Your house. You made it great, You ennobled it, and You honored it. O God, increase it in greatness, nobility, and honor. Increase its esteem and increase those who make the pilgrimage to it in goodness and nobility. O God, open to me the doors of Your mercy, let me enter Your heaven, and protect me from Satan, the accursed.

---

25 This is one of the roads leading into Mecca from the northeast.

26 Al-Bukhārī, *Ṣaḥīḥ*, 1578; Muslim, *Ṣaḥīḥ*, 1208.

27 The text of the *Iḥyāʾ* points out the difference in spelling between Kadāʾ and Kudā, and the commentary notes several variations in spelling. Al-Zabīdī, *Itḥāf*, 4:341. Kudā or Kuday road lead out of Mecca from the southeast.

28 A place north of the sacred mosque from which one could look down on the Kaʿba. The first glimpse of the Kaʿba is now from the Salām gate (Bāb al-Salām), see fig. 1.

Fifth, when he actually enters the sacred mosque (al-Masjid al-Ḥaram), he should enter through the gate of Banū Shayba,[29] and he should say,

> بسمِ اللهِ، وباللهِ، ومن اللهِ، وإلى اللهِ، وفي سبيلِ اللهِ، وعلى ملَّةِ رسولِ اللهِ صَلَّى ٱللَّهُ عَلَيْهِ وَسَلَّمَ
> In the name of God, by God, from God, to God, for the sake of God, and according to the religion of the Messenger صَلَّى ٱللَّهُ عَلَيْهِ وَسَلَّمَ of God.

And when he approaches the house, he should say,

> الحمدُ للهِ وسلامٌ على عبادِهِ الذينَ اصطفى اللّٰهُمَّ، صلِّ على محمدٍ عبدِكَ ورسولِكَ، وعلى إبراهيمَ خليلِكَ، وعلى جميعِ أنبيائِكَ ورسلِكَ
> Praise be to God and peace be on those servants He has chosen. O God, shower blessings on Muḥammad, Your servant and messenger, and on Abraham, Your intimate friend, and on all Your prophets and messengers.

Then he should raise his hands and say:

> اللّٰهُمَّ، إنِّي أسألُكَ في مَقامي هذا في أوَّلِ مناسكي أنْ تتقبَّلَ توبتي، وأنْ تتجاوزَ عَنْ خطيئتي، وتضعَ عنِّي وزرِي، الحمدُ للهِ الذي بلَّغني بيتَهُ الحرامَ الذي جعلَهُ مثابةً للناسِ وأمناً، وجعلَهُ مباركاً وهدىً للعالمينَ، اللّٰهُمَّ، إنِّي عبدُكَ، والبلدُ بلدُكَ، والحَرَمُ حرمُكَ، والبيتُ بيتُكَ، جئتُكَ أطلبُ رحمتَكَ، وأسألُكَ مسألةَ المضطرِّ الخائفِ مِنْ عقوبتِكَ، الراجي لرحمتَكَ، الطالبِ مرضاتَكَ
> O God, in this place, where my rites begin, I ask You to accept my repentance, pass over my transgressions, and lift from my shoulders the burden of my sins. Praise be to God who brought me to His sacred house that He made as a place of gathering and a refuge for humankind, who made it a blessing and a guidance for all the worlds. O God, I am Your servant, this land is Your land, this sanctuary is Your sanctuary, and this house is Your house. I come to You seeking Your mercy, and I ask You as someone in utter need, fearing Your punishment, hoping for Your mercy, and seeking what is pleasing to You.

---

29 This is the original name of the gate which is now call Bāb al-Salām ("gate of peace").

Sixth, the pilgrim should head for the black stone, touch it with his right hand, kiss it, and say,

اللّٰهُمَّ، أمانتي أديتُها، وميثاقي وفيتُهُ، اشهدْ لي بالموافاةِ

> O God, I have fulfilled my trust, I have kept my covenant. So, bear witness for me that I fulfilled it.

If he cannot kiss it, he should stand facing it and say the same.

Then nothing should interrupt him from beginning the *ṭawāf*, that is, "The circumambulation of the arrival," unless he finds the people praying an obligatory [prayer], in which case he should join them and begin the *ṭawāf* afterward.

Part 4: The Circumambulation (*Ṭawāf*)

If [the pilgrim] intends to begin the *ṭawāf*, whether it be the *ṭawāf* of arrival (*ṭawāf al-qudūm*) or any other, he must observe six acts.

First, he must observe the same conditions as for the prayer, which means, he should be free of anything that breaks the ablution, and be pure in body, clothing, and place, and cover his nakedness. For *ṭawāf* of the house is [like] prayer, but God, may He be glorified, has permitted talking during it.[30]

Before starting the *ṭawāf*, [the pilgrim] should arrange his upper garment in accordance with the task; this means fixing the [top edge] under his right armpit and then putting both ends over his left shoulder such that one end is on his back and the other on his chest.[31]

Then, on starting the *ṭawāf*, he should end the *talbiyya* and immerse himself totally in the supplications we mention later.

Second, when he finishes arranging the upper garment as described, with the house [complex] on his left and standing just before the black stone, he should leave a small space between him and it, so his whole body passes by the whole of the stone. He should leave [a space] of three paces between him and the house so that he is close to the house, which is best, but not make *ṭawāf* on the

30 That is, he should be in a state of purity, having performed the lesser ablution (*wuḍūʾ*) or the greater ablution (*ghusl*), before beginning the circumambulation.

31 This means securing the upper cloth in such as way that the right shoulder is bare.

protruding foundation stones, for they are part of the house, [even though] at the black stone, they join the ground and are [sometimes] confused with it. To walk on them invalidates the *ṭawāf* because it means that he has actually performed [part of the *ṭawāf*] inside the house, for these foundation stones are part of what remains from the original walls after they were narrowed.[32] From this place, then, the *ṭawāf* begins.

Third, at the beginning of the *ṭawāf* and before passing the black stone, he should say,

> بسم الله، والله أكبر، اللّٰهُمَّ، إيمانا بك، وتصديقا بكتابك، ووفاء بعهدك، واتباعا لسنة نبيك محمد صَلَّى ٱللَّٰهُ عَلَيْهِ وَسَلَّمَ
>
> In the name of God. God is most great. O God, [I do this] believing in You, affirming what is in Your book, in fulfillment of Your covenant, and following the *sunna* of Your Prophet Muḥammad صَلَّى ٱللَّٰهُ عَلَيْهِ وَسَلَّمَ.

He then proceeds with the *ṭawāf* and as soon as he passes the stone and comes to the door of the house, he should say,

> اللّٰهُمَّ، هذا البيت بيتك، وهذا الحرم حرمك، وهذا الأمن أمنك، وهذا مقام العائذ بك من النار
>
> O God, this house is Your house and this sanctuary is Your sanctuary, and this safety is Your safety, and this is the station of one who seeks protection in You from the fire.

When reciting the word "station" (*maqām*), he should indicate with his eyes the station[33] of Abraham عَلَيْهِ ٱلسَّلَامُ, [and then continue]:

> اللّٰهُمَّ، إن بيتك عظيم، ووجهك كريم، وأنت أرحم الراحمين، فأعذني من النار ومن الشيطان الرجيم، وحرم لحمي ودمي على النار، وآمني من أهوال يوم القيامة، واكفني مؤنة الدنيا والآخرة
>
> O God, Your house is great and Your countenance noble and You are the most Merciful of the merciful. Protect me from

---

32 These stones are now covered with polished sloping white marble which makes it impossible to mistakenly walk on them.

33 Which is to his right.

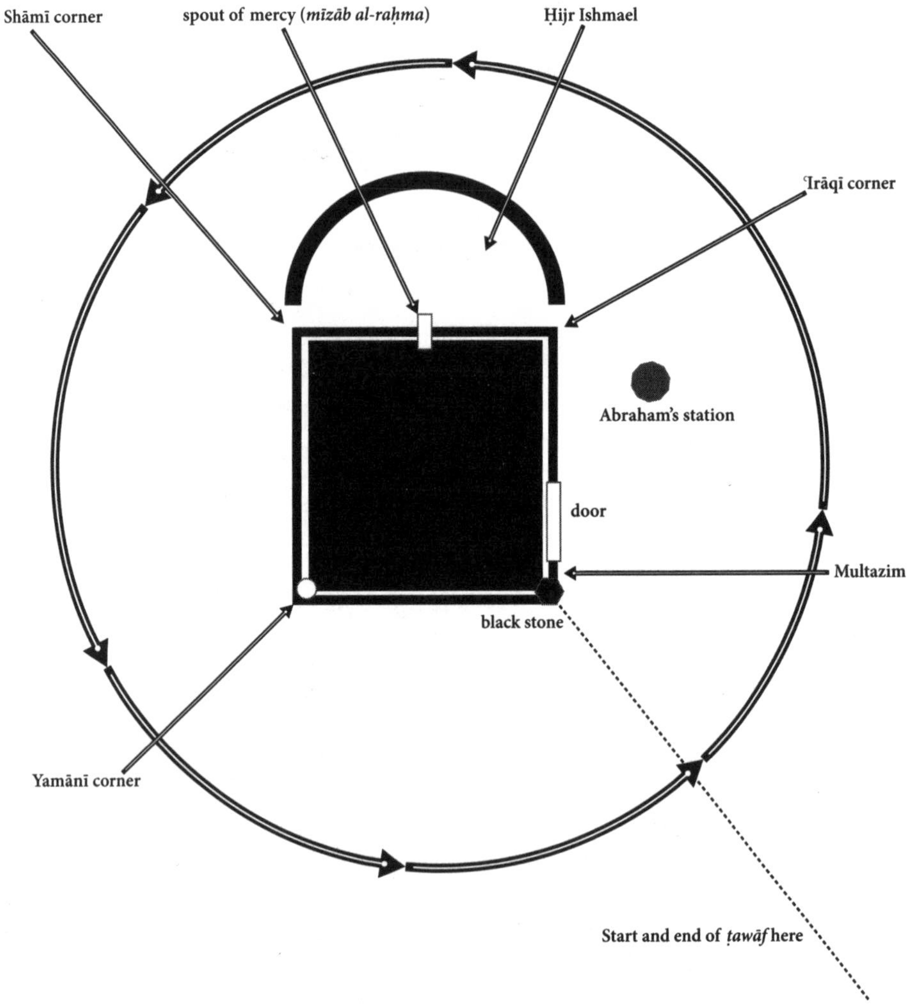

Figure 2: An approximate graphic representation of the Kaʿba showing landmarks discussed in the text. These are not to scale.

the fire and from Satan the accursed, forbid my flesh and my blood to the fire, grant me security from the calamities of the day of resurrection, and make the provisions of this world and the next sufficient for me.

Then he should glorify God and praise Him until he reaches the ʿIraqī corner,[34] where he says,

اللّٰهُمَّ، إني أعوذ بك من الشرك والشك، والكفر والنفاق، والشقاق وسوء الأخلاق، وسوء المنظر في الأهل والمال والولد

O God, I seek refuge in you from polytheism and doubt, from unbelief and hypocrisy, from schisms and vice, and from the sight of any harm to my family, wealth, and children.

When he reaches the rain spout (*mīzāb*),[35] he should say,

اللّٰهُمَّ، أظلنا تحت عرشك، يوم لا ظل إلا ظلك، اللّٰهُمَّ، اسقني بكأس محمد صَلَّى ٱللَّهُ عَلَيْهِ وَسَلَّمَ شربة، لا أظمأ بعدها أبدا

O God, shade me in the shade of Your throne on the day when there is no shade except the shade of Your throne. O God, let me drink from the cup of Muḥammad صَلَّى ٱللَّهُ عَلَيْهِ وَسَلَّمَ a drink after which I shall never thirst again.

And when he reaches the Shāmī corner, he should say,

اللّٰهُمَّ، اجعله حجا مبرورا، وسعيا مشكورا، وذنبا مغفورا، وتجارة لن تبور، يا عزيز يا غفور، رب اغفر وارحم، وتجاوز عما تعلم، إنك أنت الأعز الأكرم

O God, make this an accepted pilgrimage, an effort that earns [Your] thanks, forgiveness for my sins, and a commerce that never fails. O Almighty, O Forgiving One, Lord, forgive me, show me mercy, and pass over my sins which You know. You are the Almighty, the Generous.

When he reaches the Yamānī corner, he should say,

34 The corner of the Kaʿba after the black stone (see fig. 2).

35 This is the drain that protrudes from the roof over the north side of the Kaʿba, midway between the ʿIraqī corner and the Shāmī corner. It is also called *mīzāb al-raḥma* ("spout of mercy").

> اللَّهُمَّ، إني أعوذ بك من الكفر، وأعوذ بك من الفقر، ومن عذاب القبر، ومن فتنة المحيا والممات، وأعوذ بك من الخزي في الدنيا والآخرة
>
> O God, I seek refuge in You from disbelief, from poverty, from the punishment of the grave, and from the tribulations of life and death. I seek refuge in You from disgrace in this world and the next.

As he goes from the Yamānī corner back to the black stone, he should say,

> اللَّهُمَّ، ربنا آتنا في الدنيا حسنة، وفي الآخرة حسنة، وقنا برحمتك فتنة القبر، وعذاب النار
>
> O God, our Lord, give us goodness in this world and goodness in the next, and save us by Your mercy from the punishment of the grave and the punishment of the fire.

And when he reaches the black stone, he should say,

> اللَّهُمَّ، اغفر لي برحمتك، أعوذ برب هذا الحجر من الدين والفقر، وضيق الصدر، وعذاب القبر
>
> O God, forgive me by Your mercy. I seek refuge in the Lord of this stone from debt, poverty, vexation, and the punishment of the grave.

With this, he completes one circumambulation (*ṭawāf*). Then he repeats this circumambulation seven times in the same manner, with the [same] supplications each [time].

Fourth, he must trot (*yarmul*) in the [first] three circumambulations (*ṭawāf*) and then walk the remaining four. Here *yarmul* means "to walk quickly using short steps"; it is slower than running but faster than ordinary walking. The idea behind it and the special way the upper cloth is worn, demonstrates skill, endurance, and strength. Originally it was to discourage the disbelievers from participating in it, but it has remained a *sunna* ever since.[36]

---

36 Abū Dāwūd, *Sunan*, 1887; Ibn Mājah, *Sunan*, 2952. This is mentioned with respect to the *sunna* of trotting (without referring to the reasons), in al-Bukhārī, *Ṣaḥīḥ*, 1602; Muslim, *Ṣaḥīḥ*, 1264.

It is preferred to trot close to the house, but if that is not possible due to crowding, then trotting far from it is preferable. So, the pilgrim should go to the far edge of the area for *ṭawāf* and trot three circumambulations, then go back close to the house and the crowd and walk the remaining four.

If it is possible for him to touch the stone on each circumambulation (*ṭawāf*), it is preferable, but if he cannot because of crowding, then he should make a gesture [of touching it] with his hand and then kiss his hand. The same holds true for touching the Yamānī corner; it is recommended to touch [this corner] over the remaining corners. It is reported that the Prophet ﷺ used to touch the Yamānī corner, kiss it, and place his cheek on it.[37]

But to kiss only the [black] stone, and to greet the Yamānī corner only by touching it with the hand is preferred, since this is better-known according to what has been conveyed.[38]

Fifth, when [the pilgrim] has completed the seven circumambulations of *ṭawāf*, he should come to Multazim, which is the small area between the [black] stone and the door of the house [Kaʿba].[39] This is a place where supplications are answered,[40] so he should cling to the house, take hold of its curtains, place the front of his body against it, with his right cheek [touching] it, and his arms and palms spread out on it. Then he should say,

> اللّٰهُمَّ، يا رب البيت العتيق أعتق رقبتي من النار، وأعذني من الشيطان الرجيم، وأعذني من كل سوء، وقنعني بما رزقتني، وبارك لي فيما آتيتني، اللّٰهُمَّ، إن هذا البيت بيتك، والعبد عبدك، وهذا مقام العائذ بك من النار، اللّٰهُمَّ، اجعلني من أكرم وفدك عليك
>
> O God! O Lord of the ancient house, free me from the fire and protect me from Satan the accursed and from every evil. Let me be satisfied with what You have provided for me and blessed in what You have given me. O God, this house is Your

37 Touching the Yamānī corner is mentioned in al-Bukhārī, *Ṣaḥīḥ*, 166; Muslim, *Ṣaḥīḥ*, 1267. Kissing it is mentioned in al-Bukhārī's *Tārīkh al-kabīr*, 1:281. Placing his cheek on it is mentioned in Ibn Khuzayma, *Ṣaḥīḥ*, 2727; al-Dāraquṭnī, *Sunan*, 2:290; al-Ḥākim al-Nīsābūrī, *al-Mustadrak*, 1:456.

38 Al-Shāfiʿī, *al-Umm*, 3:430.

39 Al-Zabīdī, *Itḥāf*, 4:451.

40 Al-Azraqī, *Akhbār Makka*, 1:277.

house and this servant is Your servant, and this is the place for one who seeks refuge with You from the fire. O God, let me be among Your most excellent visitors.

Then he should praise God in abundance at this place, and invoke blessing on His Messenger ﷺ and on all the other messengers as well. He should supplicate for his personal needs, and ask forgiveness for his sins. One of the early believers used to say to his helper at this place, "Leave me alone to confess my sins to my Lord."

Sixth, when he has finished all this, [the pilgrim] should pray two cycles behind [Abraham's] station (*maqām Ibrāhīm*), reciting in the first, *Say, O disbelievers* [Q. 109] and in the second, [Sūrat] al-Ikhlāṣ [Q. 112], these being the two cycles of *ṭawāf*. Al-Zuhrī said, "The earliest *sunna* was to pray two cycles after each *ṭawāf*."[41]

But if he joins together several circumambulations and prays two cycles [for each of them], that is also allowed and was done by the Messenger ﷺ of God.

After each *ṭawāf*, which consists of seven circumambulations, and after [praying] two cycles he should make this supplication:

اللّٰهُمَّ، يسر لي اليسرى، وجنبني العسرى، واغفر لي في الآخرة والأولى، واعصمني بألطافك حتى لا أعصيك، وأعني على طاعتك بتوفيقك ،وجنبني معاصيك، واجعلني ممن يحبك، ويحب ملائكتك ورسلك، ويحب عبادك الصالحين، اللّٰهُمَّ، حببني إلى ملائكتك ورسلك، وإلى عبادك الصالحين، اللّٰهُمَّ، فكما هديتني إلى الإسلام، فثبتني عليه بألطافك، وولايتك واستعملني لطاعتك، وطاعة رسولك صَلَّى ٱللَّهُ عَلَيْهِ وَسَلَّمَ، وأجرني من مضلات الفتن

O God, ease my way to what is easy, and keep me away from what is difficult.[42] Forgive me in the next world and this one. With Your infinite kindness keep me from disobeying You, with Your accord help me to obey You, and turn me away from

41 Ibn Abī Shayba, *al-Muṣannaf*, 15058.

42 *Yassir lī-l-yusrā wa-jannibnī al-ʿusrā*, literally, "Make easy for me what is easy and keep me away from what is difficult." Commentaries on these expressions, which appear in Q. 92:7 and 92:10, say that "what is easy" is to be led to the means by which someone can accomplish good in his or her life, while the "path of difficulty" is its opposite.

disobeying You. Make me among those who love You and love Your angels, and Your messengers, and Your righteous servants, O God, and make me beloved to Your angels, Your messengers, and Your righteous servants. O God, as You have guided me to Islam, strengthen me therein with Your infinite kindness and Your protection, use me in obedience to You and to Your Messenger صَلَّىٰ ٱللَّٰهُ عَلَيۡهِ وَسَلَّمَ, and protect me from being led astray by temptation and tribulation.

Then he should return to the [black] stone, touch it, and thereby conclude the *ṭawāf*. The Prophet صَلَّىٰ ٱللَّٰهُ عَلَيۡهِ وَسَلَّمَ said, "whoever completes seven circumambulations (*ṭawāf*) of the house [Kaʿba] and then prays two cycles has the reward of someone who has freed a slave."[43] This is how the *ṭawāf* is to be done.

Of all the elements of *ṭawāf*, those which are essential, apart from the conditions of purity that apply to the prayer, are completing seven circumambulations [around] the entire house; beginning the *ṭawāf* from the black stone, placing the house [Kaʿba] on one's left; completing the *ṭawāf* in the sacred mosque [complex], but outside the house [Kaʿba] itself and therefore not on the protruding foundations nor inside [the enclosure] Ḥijr [of Ishmael/Ismāʿīl]; performing the circumambulations in succession, with no breaks between them. All other elements are *sunna* and customs.

Part 5: The Course (*Saʿī*)

WHEN [the pilgrim] has finished *ṭawāf*,[44] he should leave through Bāb al-Ṣafā, which is opposite the side of the house between the Yamānī corner and the stone.[45] Leaving from that gate, he comes to Ṣafā which is a [small] mountain.[46] This he ascends to the height of a man, for the Messenger صَلَّىٰ ٱللَّٰهُ عَلَيۡهِ وَسَلَّمَ of God ascended only far

43 Al-Tirmidhī, *Sunan*, 959; al-Nasāʾī, *Sunan*, 5:221; Ibn Mājah, *Sunan*, 2956.

44 This includes "praying two cycles, touching the black stone and the corner, and drinking water from Zamzam." Al-Zabīdī, *Itḥāf*, 4:360.

45 This is the gate immediately south of that side of the Kaʿba where walking the course (*saʿī*) begins (see fig. 1).

46 Linguistically, the word *ṣafā* is said to mean large, solid, smooth stones, and *marwā* refers to small, loose ones.

enough to see the Kaʿba.[47] To begin the course [between the two mountains] from the [actual] base of Ṣafā is sufficient, while the addition of climbing a small way up is recommended. But some steps have been added in recent times, so the pilgrim should not [mistake them for Ṣafā] and put them behind him instead [of the mountain itself], for in that case the course would be incomplete.[48] From here he starts, and then hastens between Ṣafā and Marwā seven times.

When he has gone a small way up Ṣafā, the pilgrim should turn in the direction of the house and say:

> الله أكبر، الله أكبر، الحمد لله على ما هدانا، الحمد لله بمحامده كلها، على جميع نعمه كلها، لا إله إلا الله وحده، لا شريك له، له الملك وله الحمد، يحي ويميت، بيده الخير وهو على كل شيء قدير، لا إله إلا الله وحده، صدق وعده، ونصر عبده، وأعز جنده، وهزم الأحزاب وحده، لا إله إلا الله مخلصين له الدين، ولو كره الكافرون، لا إله إلا الله مخلصين له الدين، الحمد لله رب العالمين، ﴿ فَسُبْحَـٰنَ ٱللَّهِ حِينَ تُمْسُونَ وَحِينَ تُصْبِحُونَ ﴿١٧﴾ وَلَهُ ٱلْحَمْدُ فِى ٱلسَّمَـٰوَٰتِ وَٱلْأَرْضِ وَعَشِيًّا وَحِينَ تُظْهِرُونَ ﴿١٨﴾ يُخْرِجُ ٱلْحَىَّ مِنَ ٱلْمَيِّتِ وَيُخْرِجُ ٱلْمَيِّتَ مِنَ ٱلْحَىِّ وَيُحْىِ ٱلْأَرْضَ بَعْدَ مَوْتِهَا ۚ وَكَذَٰلِكَ تُخْرَجُونَ ﴿١٩﴾ وَمِنْ ءَايَـٰتِهِۦٓ أَنْ خَلَقَكُم مِّن تُرَابٍ ثُمَّ إِذَآ أَنتُم بَشَرٌ تَنتَشِرُونَ ﴿٢٠﴾ ﴾ اللهم، إني أسألك إيمانا دائما، ويقينا صادقا، وعلما نافعا، وقلبا خاشعا، ولسانا ذاكرا، وأسألك العفو والعافية، والمعافاة الدائمة، في الدنيا والآخرة
>
> God is most great. Praise be to God for all that to which He has guided us. Praise be to God through all His forms of praise for the totality of His blessings. There is no god but God, the One, without partner. His is the kingdom and His [is] the praise, He gives life and causes death, in His hand is all good, and He has power over all things. There is no god but God, the One, without partner. He has been true to His promise, given victory to His servant, and honored His forces.

47 Muslim, *Ṣaḥīḥ*, 1218, in part of a long *ḥadīth*.

48 The steps were a structure in Imām al-Ghazālī's time; here he advises pilgrims to start the course properly at the actual base of the mountian and not on any added structure.

> He alone has defeated the clans.[49] There is no god but God. Our *dīn* is totally for Him, though disbelievers may be averse. There is no god but God. Our *dīn* is totally for Him. Praise be to God, Lord of the worlds. *So exalted is God when you reach the evening and when you reach the morning. And to Him is* [*due all*] *praise throughout the heavens and the earth. And* [*exalted is He*] *at night and when you are at noon. He brings the living out of the dead and brings the dead out of the living and brings to life the earth after its lifelessness. And thus will you be brought out. And of His signs is that He created you from dust; then, suddenly you were human beings dispersing* [*throughout the earth*] [Q. 30:17–20]. O God, I ask You for enduring faith, true certitude, beneficial knowledge, a reverent heart, and a supplicating tongue. I ask You for pardon, well-being, and mutual clemency in this world and the next.

He should then invoke God's blessings on Muḥammad ﷺ and end by supplicating God for his personal needs.

He then descends [the mountain] and begins the course saying,

> رب اغفر وارحم، وتجاوز عما تعلم، إنك أنت الأعز الأكرم، اللّٰهُمَّ آتنا في الدنيا حسنة، وفي الآخرة حسنة، وقنا عذاب النار
>
> O Lord! Forgive me, show me mercy, pardon me for what You know [of my sins], You are the almighty and the most generous. O God, give us goodness in this world and goodness in the hereafter, and save us from the punishment of the fire.

He sets out walking at a normal pace until he comes to the green slope (*al-mayl al-akhḍār*) which is situated at the corner of the sacred mosque [and is] the first of what he comes to on descending from Ṣafā. When there remain about six cubits (shoulder lengths) between him and the slope in front of him, he should break into

49 This refers to the battle of the trench (in 5/627) in which the Prophet was victorious over the confederacy of Arab tribes (hence clans). For the Qurʾānic account, see 33:9–27. For *sīra* accounts, see al-Mubarakpuri, *ar-Raheeq al-makhtūm*, 311–324, Lings, *Muhammad*, 215–219.

a trot, referred to as *ramal*, and continue this until he has reached the [other side of the slope], where he should resume walking.[50]

When he reaches Marwā, he should climb [a little way] up as he did at Ṣafā and, facing Ṣafā utter the same invocation [used there]. This completes one (length) of the course, and when he returns to Ṣafā, two are complete. He must complete seven [of these laps], trotting up and down the green slope and walking for the remainder, and stopping and slightly ascending Ṣafā or Marwā each time.

When he has finished, [then] he has completed the *ṭawāf* of arrival and the course, both of which are *sunna*. It is preferable to be in a state of purity for the course, but it is not obligatory, as it is for the *ṭawāf*.

If he performs the course [once], he should not perform it again after the standing [at ʿArafa], but rather accept it as a completed pillar. For it is not a precondition that the course be delayed [until after] the standing [at ʿArafa], although it is a precondition for the obligatory circumambulation.

However, a precondition for any performance of the course is that it follow the *ṭawāf*.

Part 6: The Standing (*Wuqūf*) at ʿArafa and What Precedes It

If the pilgrim reaches ʿArafa on the day of ʿArafa, then he does not spend time doing the *ṭawāf* of arrival and entering Mecca before [he goes to do] the standing. If he arrives some days before that, however, then he should complete the *ṭawāf* of arrival and remain in *iḥrām* until the seventh day of Dhū l-Ḥijja.[51] On that day, the *imām* in Mecca delivers a sermon after the midday [prayer] at the Kaʿba. In the sermon he orders the people to prepare for the

---

50 *Al-mayl al-akhḍar* was originally a depression in the ground, roughly midway between the two mountains. It is said that here, when Hagar went between the two hills, she lost sight of her baby Ishmael (whom she had placed in a slight depression on the ground of Ṣafā), so she ran to the other side so she could see him again. The whole course between Ṣafā and Marwā is now enclosed and is at ground level with the mosque and the place for trotting is marked by green lamps on either side.

51 Unless he had intended to first complete the visit (*ʿumra*) following the third method (*tamattauʿ*) described earlier.

journey to Minā[52] on the day of *tarwiyya*,[53] to spend a night there, and then, the following morning, to make their way to ʿArafa in order to fulfill the obligation of standing, starting just after midday. The time for standing is from just after midday [of the ninth] until the true dawn on the day of sacrifice. The pilgrims should go down to Minā reciting the *talbiyya*, and it is recommended that, if he can, [the pilgrim] should go from Mecca on foot to complete the [remaining] rites of the pilgrimage. Walking from the mosque of Abraham عَلَيْهِ ٱلسَّلَامُ to the place of the standing [at ʿArafa] is especially meritorious and affirmed [as a *sunna*].

Upon reaching Minā, he should say, "O God, this is Minā! Bestow on me what You have bestowed on Your friends (*umnun ʿalaya bimā mananta bihi ʿalā awliyāʾik*)[54] and those obedient to You." He should stay that night at Minā, which in itself is just a place to camp the nights; it is not connected to a rite.

When he awakens on the morning of ʿArafa [10 Dhū l-Ḥijja], he should first offer the dawn prayer. Then, when the sun has risen on Thabīr,[55] he should set out for ʿArafa, saying,

اللّٰهُمَّ، اجعلها خير غدوة غدوتها قط، وأقربها من رضوانك، وأبعدها من سخطك، اللّٰهُمَّ، إليك غدوت، وإياك رجوت، وعليك اعتمدت، ووجهك أردت، فاجعلني ممن تباهي به اليوم من هو خير مني وأفضل

52 A valley about five miles from the sacred mosque.

53 *Yawm al-tarwiyya* is the eighth day of Dhū l-Ḥijja, the night of which is spent at Minā. The name *tarwiyya* is said to be derived from the verb *rawiya* ("to give water to someone or something") because on this day pilgrims in earliest times would drink their fill of water in Mecca because they were heading for Minā, where there might not be any. An alternative explanation puts the origin of *tarwiyya* in the verb *raʾā* ("to see"), in reference to Abraham's vision of sacrificing his son, which is said to have happened on the eve of the eighth day. According to these sources, he first asked himself whether the vision was from God or from Satan. When the same dream reappeared the next night, the eve of the tenth, "he woke up and knew (*ʿarafa*) it was true, and so that day was called ʿArafa." See al-Thaʿlabī, *Tafsīr*, 2:198–203, and al-Baghwī, *Maʿālim al-tanzīl*, on the same verses. Also see al-Qurṭubī, *Jāmiʿ aḥkām al-Qurʾān*, on 37:102–113.

54 This supplication shows the linguistic connection between the name Minā and the verb *manna*, "to give as a blessing or gift." The noun, *mannā*, is also the name of the food sent from heaven ("manna") to the children of Israel. It is mentioned in the Old Testament (Exodus 16) and in the Qurʾān (2:57).

55 A mountain about one and one-half miles east of Mecca; it is visible from Minā.

> O God, make this the best morning journey I have ever taken, the one that brings me closest to what is pleasing to You and furthest from what incurs Your wrath. O God, to You I set out this morning, in You I place my hope, on You I depend, and for Your countenance I wish. Today make me among those of whom You boast to those who are better and more excellent than I.[56]

Arriving at ʿArafa, he should pitch his tent at Namra near the mosque, for this is where the Messenger صَلَّى ٱللَّهُ عَلَيْهِ وَسَلَّمَ of God pitched a round tent (*qubba*).[57] Namra is in [the valley of] ʿUrna, which is below the place of standing and ʿArafa.

Then he should perform the greater ablution for the standing. After the sun has passed the meridian, the *imām* delivers a brief sermon and is then seated; the muezzin gives the call to prayer; and the *imām* [then] starts a second sermon. The call just before the prayer (*iqāma*) is made immediately following the call to prayer, and the *imām* finishes [his sermon] just as the *iqāma* finishes. He then offers the midday (*ẓuhr*) and afternoon (*ʿaṣr*) prayers together so that there is one single call to prayer (*adhān*) but a call to stand (*iqāma*) for prayer before each. These are then prayed in the shortened form [of two cycles each]. Following this, the pilgrim should head to the place of standing at ʿArafa, where the standing [begins, making sure that he does] not do [this] in the valley of ʿUrna.

[We specify this] because the front of the mosque of Abraham عَلَيْهِ ٱلسَّلَامُ is actually in the valley [of ʿUrna] and the back is in ʿArafa. So, if someone stands in front of the mosque, he will not have completed the standing at ʿArafa. The site of ʿArafa is marked to distinguish it from the mosque by some large rocks spread out there. It is best to stand close to the *imām*, face the *qibla*, and sit on one's mount.[58]

The pilgrim should [express] various formulas of praise and glorification, affirm [his] faith, praise God عَزَّوَجَلَّ, supplicate to Him,

---

56 This is a reference to the angels.

57 As is related in Muslim, *Ṣaḥīḥ*, 1218.

58 There are numerous sound *ḥadīth*s describing the Prophet صَلَّى ٱللَّهُ عَلَيْهِ وَسَلَّمَ on his camel at ʿArafa. However, the commentary points out that this does not imply that being at ʿArafa mounted is superior to being there on foot. Al-Zabīdī, *Itḥāf*, 4:371.

and repent in abundance.[59] He should not fast this day so as to have enough strength to continue his supplications, nor should he stop reciting the *talbiyya* on the day of ʿArafa. Rather, it is most beloved for the pilgrim to spend part of the time reciting the *talbiyya* and part of the time absorbed in supplications.

He should not depart from the area of ʿArafa until after sunset so that he might spend a day and a night there. If it is possible for him to stand there for some time on the eighth [of Dhū l-Ḥijja], in case of some error in [sighting] the crescent moon,[60] this would be a precaution and safer [than possibily] missing the standing, for whoever misses standing at ʿArafa until the break of dawn on the day of sacrifice has missed the entire pilgrimage. [In that case,] he must leave his *iḥrām* by completing the rites of the visit, offer a sacrifice because of what he missed, and fulfill the duty of pilgrimage the following year.

Supplications should be the main concern of [the pilgrim at ʿArafa], for on that day, in such a place, and in such a gathering, he can be hopeful that his prayers will be answered.

Supplications transmitted from the Messenger ﷺ of God and from the early believers are the best to use on the day of ʿArafa. [A pilgrim] should say

> لا إله إلا الله وحده، لا شريك له، له الملك، وله الحمد، يحيي ويميت، وهو حي لا يموت، بيده الخير، وهو على كل شيء قدير.
>
> There is no god but God, alone without partner; His is the kingdom and He is the one we praise; He gives life, and He causes death; He is the Living who never dies; in His hand is all good and He has power, over all things.[61]

> اللَّهُمَّ، اجعل في قلبي نوراً، وفي سمعي نوراً، وفي بصري نوراً، وفي لساني نوراً، اللَّهُمَّ اشرح لي صدري، ويسر لي أمري.

---

59 The commentary adds, "This is a place for humility and weeping… It is related in al-Ṭabarānī, *al-Muʿjam al-awsaṭ*, 2913, that Ibn ʿAbbās said, 'I saw the Prophet ﷺ making supplications standing at ʿArafa with his hand on his breast like a poor man asking for food.'" Al-Zabīdī, *Itḥāf*, 4:371.

60 The crescent moon that marks the beginning of Dhū l-Ḥijja.

61 Al-Tirmidhī, *Sunan*, 3585; Mālik, *al-Muwaṭṭaʾ*, 1:322.

O God, put light in my heart, light in my hearing, light in my vision, and light in my tongue. O God, expand my breast and make my situation easy for me.[62]

Then he should say,

اللّٰهُمَّ، رب الحمد، لك الحمد كما تقول، وخيرا مما نقول، لك صلاتي ونسكي ومحياي ومماتي، وإليك مآبي وإليك ثوابي، اللّٰهُمَّ، إني أعوذ بك من وساوس الصدر، وشتات الأمر، وعذاب القبر؛ اللّٰهُمَّ، إني أعوذ بك من شر ما يلج في الليل، ومن شر ما يلج في النهار، ومن شر ما تهب به الرياح، ومن شر بوائق الدهر

O God, Lord of praise! Yours are the praises we and those better than us say. Yours is my prayer and my sacrifice, my life and my death, to You is my retreat, and to You my return. O God, I truly seek refuge in You from whisperings [in my] breast, from [my] matters falling apart, and from the punishment of the grave. O God, I truly seek refuge in You from the evil of that which enters into the night, and from the evil of that which enters into the daylight, and from the evil of that which is carried by the winds, and from the calamities of time.[63]

اللّٰهُمَّ إني أعوذ بك من تحول عافيتك، وفجأة نقمتك، وجميع سخطك

O God, I seek refuge in You from turning away the well-being You have granted me, from being suddenly seized by Your punishment, and from all that [merits] Your wrath.[64]

اللّٰهُمَّ، اهدني بالهدى، واغفر لي في الآخرة والأولى، يا خير مقصود وأسنى منزول به، وأكرم مسئول ما لديه، أعطني العشية أفضل ما أعطيت أحدا من خلقك، وحجاج بيتك، يا أرحم الراحمين؛ اللّٰهُمَّ، يا رفيع الدرجات، ومنزل البركات، ويا فاطر الأرضين والسموات، ضجت إليك الأصوات، بصنوف اللغات، يسألونك الحاجات، وحاجتي إليك أن لا تنساني في دار البلاء إذا نسيني أهل الدنيا

---

62   Al-Bayhaqī, *al-Sunan al-kubrā*, 5:117.
63   Al-Tirmidhī, *Sunan*, 3530, with similar wording.
64   Muslim, *Ṣaḥīḥ*, 3739

O God, guide me with guidance and forgive me in the hereafter and the present.[65] You are the best of all that I seek, the most bounteous of all with whom I might reside, the most generous of any whom I might ask. On this evening give me the best of that which You have given to any of Your creatures and pilgrims of Your house, O Most Merciful of the merciful! O God, You have the highest of ranks, and You are the one who causes blessings to descend. O Fashioner of the earths and heavens! Voices cry out to You in every tongue asking You [to fulfill their] needs, and my need before You is that You not forget me in this, the abode of trials and afflictions, when the people of the world have forgotten me.[66]

اللَّهُمَّ، إنك تسمع كلامي، وترى مكاني، وتعلم سري وعلانيتي، ولا يخفى عليك شيء من أمري، أنا البائس الفقير، المستغيث المستجير، الوجل المشفق، المعترف بذنبه، أسألك مسألة المسكين، وأبتهل إليك ابتهال المذنب الذليل، وأدعوك دعاء الخائف الضرير، دعاء من خضعت لك رقبته، وفاضت لك عبرته، وذل لك جسده، ورغم لك أنفه؛ اللَّهُمَّ، لا تجعلني بدعائك رب شقيا، وكن بي رءوفا رحيما، يا خير المسئولين، وأكرم المعطين

O God, You hear my words and You see my place and You know both what I conceal and what I reveal, and none of my cares is hidden from You. I am [of] *the miserable and poor* [22:28], someone who seeks Your aid and refuge, someone full of fear and dread, acknowledging my sins. I pray to You in my utter need, I beseech You as a lowly sinner, and call on You with the call of someone blind and afraid, of someone who completely surrenders to You, with tears overflowing, body humbled before You, abased before You. O God, do not make me, *in my prayer to You unhappy*.[67] Be clement and compassionate toward me. You are the best of any we can ask, and most generous of all those who give.

---

65 Al-Ṭabarānī, *al-Duʿāʾ*, 878.

66 Abū Nuʿaym, *Ḥilya*, 7:275.

67 This is an allusion to the Qurʾān: *and never have I been in my supplication to You, my Lord, unhappy* [19:4], quoting the supplication of Zachariah (Zakariyyāʾ).

إلهي، من مدح لك نفسه، فإني لائم نفسي

My God! While some praise themselves before You, I blame myself before You.

إلهي، أخرست المعاصي لساني، فما لي وسيلة عن عمل، ولا شفيع سوى الأمل

My God! Sins have silenced my tongue, I have no means through my deeds, and no intercessor except hope.

إلهي، إني أعلم أن ذنوبي لم تبق لي عندك جاها، ولا للاعتذار وجها، ولكنك أكرم الأكرمين

My God! I know so well that my sins have left me without any standing before You, nor have I any basis for excuse, but You are the Most Generous of the generous.

إلهي، إن لم أكن أهلا أن أبلغ رحمتك، فإن رحمتك أهل أن تبلغني، ورحمتك وسعت كل شيء، وأنا شيء

My God! I do not deserve to reach Your mercy, yet Your mercy deserves to reach me, for Your mercy surrounds all things, and I am one of those things.[68]

إلهي، إن ذنوبي وإن كانت عظاما، ولكنها صغار في جنب عفوك، فاغفرها لي يا كريم

My God! Though my sins are huge, they are small when compared to Your pardon, so forgive me, O God most generous.

إلهي، أنت أنت وأنا أنا، أنا العواد إلى الذنوب، وأنت العواد إلى المغفرة

My God! You are You and I am I, and even as I sin again and again, You forgive again and again.

إلهي، إن كنت لا ترحم إلا أهل طاعتك، فإلى من يفزع المذنبون

My God! If Your mercy were only for the obedient, then to whom would sinners turn?

---

68 Abū Nuʿaym, *Ḥilya*, 5:298.

إلهي، تجنبت عن طاعتك عمدا، وتوجهت إلى معصيتك قصدا، فسبحانك ما أعظم حجتك علي، وأكرم عفوك عني، فبوجوب حجتك علي، وانقطاع حجتي عنك، وفقري إليك، وغناك عني إلا غفرت لي

My God! I have intentionally turned away from obeying You and intentionally turned in the direction of sin. Glory be to You! How great is Your proof against me, and how generous Your clemency toward me! By the certainty of Your proof against me and the futility of my excuses before You, by my need for You and Your independence of me—by all that, forgive me.[69]

يا خير من دعاه داع، وأفضل من رجاه راج، بحرمة الإسلام، وبذمة محمد ﷺ أتوسل إليك، فاغفر لي جميع ذنوبي، واصرفني من موقفي هذا مقضي الحوائج، وهب لي ما سألت، وحقق رجائي فيما تمنيت

O [You who are the] best of those to whom any supplicant may call, and most excellent of those from whom anyone may hope for goodness, by the sanctity of Islam and the promise of Muḥammad ﷺ, I call on You. Forgive me all my sins and send me from this place of standing with my needs fulfilled. Bestow on me what I ask, and realize my hope as I have hoped.

إلهي، دعوتك بالدعاء الذي علمتنيه، فلا تحرمني الرجاء الذي عرفتنيه

My God! I have called to You with the supplication that you have taught me, so do not forbid me the hope which You have allowed me to have.

إلهي، ما أنت صانع العشية بعبد مقر لك بذنبه، خاشع لك بذلته، مستكين بجرمه، متضرع إليك من عمله، تائب إليك من اقترافه، مستغفر لك من ظلمه، مبتهل إليك في العفو عنه، طالب إليك نجاح حوائجه، راج إليك في موقفه، مع كثرة ذنوبه، فيا ملجأ كل حي، وولي كل مؤمن، من أحسن فبرحمتك يفوز، ومن أخطأ فبخطيئته يهلك

69 Abū Nuʿaym, *Ḥilya*, 7:304.

My God! What will You do this evening with a servant confessing to You his sins, coming humbly before You, abased by his transgressions, begging You with his paltry and defective deeds, seeking repentance for his transgressions, asking Your forgiveness for his wrongs, begging Your pardon of him, seeking Your satisfaction of his needs, and ever hopeful of You in this place of standing even with the multitude of his sins. O You who are the shelter for every living thing, the protecting friend of every faithful servant, whoever does well by Your mercy succeeds, and whoever does badly by his transgressions perishes.

اللّٰهُمَّ، إليك خرجنا، وبفنائك أنخنا، وإياك أملنا، وما عندك طلبنا، ولإحسانك تعرضنا، ورحمتك رجونا، ومن عذابك أشفقنا، وإليك بأثقال الذنوب هربنا، ولبيتك الحرام حججنا، يا من، يملك حوائج السائلين، ويعلم ضمائر الصامتين، يا من، ليس معه رب يدعى، ويا من، ليس فوقه خالق يخشى، ويا من، ليس له وزير يؤتي، ولا حاجب يرشى، يا من، لا يزداد على كثرة السؤال إلا جودا وكرما، وعلى كثرة الحوائج إلا تفضلا وإحسانا

O God! To You we have come out, and in this, Your vast open place, our camels kneel, for You alone we hope, we seek what is with You, to Your generosity and goodness we open ourselves, for Your compassion we hope, and Your punishment we dread; to You we escape from the burden of sin, and to Your sacred house we have made pilgrimage. O God, You possess all that those who pray to You need, You know the minds of those who do not speak, beside You there is no other Lord to whom we call, above You there is no other creator to be feared. O God, You have no vizier to ask nor gatekeeper to bribe, and You do not respond to the many supplications except with generosity and munificence, nor to the abundance of needs except with excellence and goodness.[70]

---

70 Ibn ʿAbd al-Barr conveyed a supplication like this in *Bahjat al-majālis* (2:271) on the authority of al-Aṣmaʿī.

اللّهُمَّ، إنك جعلت لكل ضيف قرى، ونحن أضيافك، فاجعل قرانا منك الجنة
O God! You have made for every guest a feast of welcome, and we are Your guests, so let our feast from You be heaven.[71]

اللّهُمَّ، إن لكل وفد جائزة، ولكل زائر كرامة، ولكل سائل عطية، ولكل راج ثوابا، ولكل ملتمس لم عندك جزاء، ولكل مسترحم عندك رحمة، ولكل راغب إليك زلفى، ولكل متوسل إليك عفوا، وقد وفدنا إلى بيتك الحرام، ووقفنا بهذه المشاعر العظام، وشهدنا هذه المشاهد الكرام، رجاء لما عندك، فلا تخيب رجاءنا
O God! For every delegate there is a present; for every visitor, an act of kindness; for every petitioner, a gift; for everyone hopeful, some reward; for everyone who comes seeking Your presence, satisfaction; and for everyone who comes seeking Your mercy, mercy; for all who come desiring You, nearness; and for all those who pray to You, pardon. We have come as visitors to Your sacred house and have stood at these holy sites and been present in these noble shrines hoping for Your favor, so do not disappoint us.

إلهنا، تابعت النعم، حتى اطمأنت الأنفس بتتابع نعمك، وأظهرت العبر، حتى نطقت الصوامت بحجتك، وظاهرت المنن، حتى اعترف أولياؤك بالتقصير عن حقك، وأظهرت الآيات، حتى أفصحت السموات والأرضون بأدلتك، وقهرت بقدرتك، حتى خضع كل شيء لعزتك، وعنت الوجوه لعظمتك، إذا أساءت عبادك، حلمت وأمهلت، وإن أحسنوا، تفضلت وقبلت، وإن عصوا، سترت، وإن أذنبوا، عفوت وغفرت، وإذا دعونا، أجبت، وإذا نادينا، سمعت، وإذا أقبلنا إليك، قربت، وإذا ولينا عنك، دعوت
Our God, You have blessed us so continually that our souls have found peace in the constant flow of Your blessings. You have shown us so many lessons in creation that even the speechless bear witness, You have manifested so many instances of Your grace that even Your saints acknowledge their shortcomings in fulfilling [the gratitude] due You; You have revealed so many signs that even the heavens and the earths pronounce Your proof; and You have overwhelmed

71 Al-Dīnawarī, *al-Majālisa wa-jawāhir al-ʿilm*, 23.

with Your power until all creatures yield before Your might; and faces are humbled before Your grandeur. If Your servants do wrong, You are gentle and give respite; and if they do well, show them favor and accept them; if they disobey, You conceal; and if they sin, You forgive and forgive. If we pray to You, You listen; if we call to You, You hear; if we turn in Your direction, You draw near; and if we turn away from You, You call us back!

إلهنا، إنك قلت في كتابك المبين، لمحمد خاتم النبيين، قُل لِّلَّذِينَ كَفَرُوٓاْ إِن يَنتَهُواْ يُغْفَرْ لَهُم مَّا قَدْ سَلَفَ، فأرضاك عنهم بالإقرار بكلمة التوحيد بعد الجحود، وإنا نشهد لك بالتوحيد مخبتين، ولمحمد بالرسالة مخلصين، فاغفر لنا بهذه الشهادة سوالف الإجرام، ولا تجعل حظنا فيه أنقص من حظ من دخل في الإسلام

Our God! You have said in Your clear book to Muḥammad the seal of the prophets, *Say to those who have disbelieved* [*that*] *if they cease, what has previously occurred will be forgiven for them* [8:38], so You accepted them simply by their affirmation of the statement of unity (*tawḥīd*), after [they had] repudiated it. We bear witness to Your unity in humility and to the message of Muḥammad with sincerity, so with this testimony forgive us our previous sins and let not our portion [of Your mercy] be less than [Your mercy for] those who entered Islam.

إلهنا، إنك أحببت التقرب إليك بعتق ما ملكت أيماننا، ونحن عبيدك، وأنت أولى بالتفضل فاعتقنا، وإنك أمرتنا أن نتصدق على فقرائنا ونحن فقراؤك، وأنت أحق بالتطول فتصدق علينا، ووصيتنا بالعفو عمن ظلمنا وقد ظلمنا أنفسنا، وأنت أحق بالكرم فاعف عنا، ربنا اغفر لنا، وارحمنا، أنت مولانا، رَبَّنَآ ءَاتِنَا فِى ٱلدُّنْيَا حَسَنَةً وَفِى ٱلْأٓخِرَةِ حَسَنَةً وَقِنَا عَذَابَ ٱلنَّارِ ﴿٢٠١﴾

Our God! You love those who draw near You by setting free the slaves they have owned, and here we are, Your slaves, and You are the best to show favor, so set us free. And You have commanded us to be charitable toward the poor, and here we are, Your poor, and You are the most entitled to show

> generosity, so be charitable toward us. And You have enjoined us to forgive those who wrong us. And here we are, having wronged our own souls, and You are the most entitled to act nobly, so pardon us. Forgive us, Our Lord, and have mercy on us, our Protector. *Our Lord, give us in this world* [*that which is*] *good and in the hereafter* [*that which is*] *good and protect us from the punishment of the fire* [2:201].

He should also frequently use the supplication of Khiḍr عَلَيْهِ ٱلسَّلَامُ:

> يا من، لا يشغله شأن عن شأن، ولا سمع عن سمع، ولا تشتبه عليه الأصوات، يا من، لا تغلطه المسائل، ولا تختلف عليه اللغات، يا من، لا يبرمه إلحاح الملحين، ولا تضجره مسألة السائلين، أذقنا برد عفوك، وحلاوة مناجاتك
>
> O You who are not diverted from one concern to another, You hear [one voice] without being diverted from hearing another, the many voices [calling on You] are each distinct, and You do not mistake any of the many supplicants, nor any of the many languages. O You who are never repulsed by the importuning of those who importune, and never vexed by the supplications of all who supplicate You. Let us taste the coolness of Your pardon and the sweetness of Your mercy.[72]

He should then supplicate in whatever way occurs to him, and ask forgiveness for himself, his parents, and all the faithful men and women. He should be insistent in his supplications and give importance to what he is asking from God, for with God nothing is too great.

Once while at ʿArafa, Muṭarrif b. ʿAbdallāh said "O God, do not refuse all these people because of me!"[73]

And Bakr al-Muzanī said, "A man said, 'When I looked on the people at ʿArafa, I thought that they might all have been forgiven had I not been among them.'"[74]

---

72 Al-Dīnawarī, *al-Majālis wa-jawāhir al-ʿilm*, 23; al-Khaṭīb al-Baghdādī, *Tārīkh Baghdād*, 4:340; Ibn ʿAsākir, *Tārīkh madinat Dimashq*, 19:325.

73 Ibn al-Jawzī, *Ṣifat al-ṣafwa*, 3:119.

74 Al-Bayhaqī, *Shuʿab al-īmān*, 7902, 7903.

Part 7: On the Remaining Rites of the Pilgrimage after the Standing [at ʿArafa]: Camping [on Minā], Casting [the Pebbles], Making the Sacrifice, Cutting the Hair, and the [Final] *Ṭawāf*

WHEN [the pilgrim] goes forth from ʿArafa after sunset, he should do so calmly and with dignity and avoid galloping the horses and the camels as some people are wont to do, for the Messenger ﷺ of God prohibited this, saying "Fear God, go forth with beauty, and do not tread on a weak [person], nor harm a Muslim."[75]

Then when [the pilgrim] reaches Muzdalifa he must perform the greater ablution (*ghusl*), because Muzdalifa is a part of the sanctuary, so he should enter it clean. If he is able to enter on foot, it is better [to do so] and more respectful of the sanctuary, and he should raise his voice [recite] the *talbiyya* as he goes along the road.

When he reaches Muzdalifa, he should say,

اللّٰهُمَّ، إن هذه مزدلفة، جمعت فيها ألسنة مختلفة، تسألك حوائج مؤتنفة، فاجعلني ممن دعاك فاستجبت له، وتوكل عليك فكفيته

> O God, this is Muzdalifa where so many gather [speaking in] diverse tongues, calling on You; let me be among those who supplicate to You and whose [supplications You] accept, [among those who] trust in You and were sufficed.

Then, there in Muzdalifa, he should combine and shorten [the prayers after] sunset (*maghrib*) and night (*ʿishāʾ*)[76] at the time of the night prayer. There should be one call to prayer (*adhān*) and two calls to stand for the prayer (*iqāmatayn*) without any supererogatory [prayer] (*nāfila*) between them. Rather, he should combine the supererogatory [prayer] of *maghrib* and *ʿishāʾ* with the odd-numbered *witr* [prayer] after the two obligatory [prayers]. He begins with the supererogatory [prayer] of *maghrib*, and the supererogatory [prayer] of *ʿishāʾ*, as [one does while] traveling. Indeed, omitting these supererogatory [prayers] while traveling is

75 Al-Bukhārī, *Ṣaḥīḥ*, 1671; Abū Dāwūd, *Sunan*, 1920; al-Nasāʾī, *Sunan*, 5:257.

76 As in a traveler's prayer, with the four cycles of the night prayer reduced to two.

an evident loss, but to insist that they be done at fixed times is a hardship and therefore removes the necessity that they be prayed after the obligatory [prayer]. Indeed, if it is permissible to make the dry ablution (*tayammum*) once to pray the supererogatory prayers together with obligatory ones in accordance with the rule of priority,[77] then it is even more permissible to combine them in accordance with the same rule. And this separation between the obligatory [prayers] and the supererogatory ones [which normally follow them] is not affected by the fact that it is permissible to perform [the supererogatory prayer] while riding, because of what we have already pointed out with respect to priority and need.

[The pilgrim] then spends that night at Muzdalifa. Since camping there is considered part of the rites, whoever leaves in the first half of the night and does not spend the night there must make amends by sacrificing [an animal]. For those who can manage it, keeping a vigil during that exalted night is among the best ways of drawing near to God.

When half the night has passed, the pilgrim should prepare for his departure, taking with him some pebbles from [Muzdalifa], for the pebbles there are smooth. He should take seventy of these, the [exact] quantity required, but there is no harm in having more on hand,[78] for he may drop some on the way. The pebbles should be light enough to hold with the fingers [of one hand].

Then he should offer the dawn (*fajr*) prayer [while it is still] dark, and walk until he reaches the sacred monument (*al-mashʿar al-ḥaram*) which is at the end of Muzdalifa.

He should stop there and make supplications until the sky shows the first glow of dawn, saying,

> اللّهُمَّ، بحق المشعر الحرام، والبيت الحرام، والشهر الحرام، والركن والمقام، أبلغ روح محمد منا التحية والسلام، وأدخلنا دار السلام، يا ذا الجلال والإكرام
>
> O God, by the right of the sacred monument and the sacred house and the sacred month and the corner and the station

---

77 By which he means that if a traveler makes the dry ablution (*tayammum*) for an obligatory prayer, then he is permitted to offer a supererogatory prayer following it without renewing the dry ablution.

78 The number of pebbles required at the first pillar is seven. Here, however, al-Ghazālī is noting the number of pebbles needed for all three pillars for the three days following.

> [of Abraham], convey from us to the spirit of Muḥammad greetings and salutations of peace and let us enter the abode of peace, O You [who are] endowed with majesty and generosity.[79]

He then continues from there before sunrise until he reaches a place called Wādī Muḥassir. There it recommended that he should speed up his mount as he passes through the valley or, if he is on foot, quicken his pace.

Then, on the morning of the day of sacrifice, he should begin mixing the *talbiyya* with the *takbīr*,[80] repeating them alternately, until he reaches Minā and the places of pillars (*jamarāt*), which are three in number. He [should] pass by the first and the second of these, for they are of no concern on the day of sacrifice, and he [should] go on to the third pillar (*al-jamarat al-ʿAqaba*), which is on the right when facing the direction of prayer, on the main road. The place for throwing [the pebbles] is slightly elevated on the slope of the mountain, above the places of the pillars, and there, after the sun has risen the height of a spear above the horizon, he should cast his pebbles. The best way to do this is while facing the direction of prayer, although there is no harm if he is facing the pillar itself. Then he [should] throw seven pebbles, raising his hand to do so, and uttering the *takbīr*, not the *talbiyya*. Thus, on throwing each pebble, he should say,

> الله أكبر، على طاعة الرحمن، ورغم الشيطان، اللَّهُمَّ تصديقا بكتابك، واتباعا لسنة نبيك
>
> God is greater! [I do this] in obedience to the All-Merciful, and in defiance of Satan. O God, [I do this] affirming my belief in Your book and following the *sunna* of Your Prophet.[81]

When he has thrown [all seven], he should cease all [recitation of] the *talbiyya* and the *takbīr*, except for the repetition of the *takbīr* following each of the obligatory prayers, starting with the midday prayer (*ẓuhr*) on the day of sacrifice, and [ending with] the dawn (*fajr*) prayer on the last of the days of *tashrīq*.[82] Also, he should not

---

79 Abū Shaykh, *Ṭabaqāt al-muḥaddithīn*, 331, with wording close to this but not particular to Muzdalifa.

80 That is, the words *Allāhu akbar* (God is greater).

81 Ibn Abī Shayba, *al-Muṣannaf*, 16045; al-Bayhaqī, *al-Sunan al-kubrā*, 5:79.

82 The three days (11–13 Dhū l-Ḥijja) following the day of the sacrifice (*ʿīd al-adḥā*).

stay [at the pillar] for supplications on this day. Rather, he should make supplications in his home.

The formula of *takbīr* is as follows:

> الله أكبر، الله أكبر، الله أكبر كبيرا، والحمد لله كثيرا، وسبحان الله بكرة وأصيلا، لا إله إلا الله وحده، لا شريك له، مخلصين له الدين، ولو كره الكافرون، لا إله إلا الله وحده، صدق وعده، ونصر عبده، وهزم الأحزاب وحده، لا إله إلا الله، والله أكبر
>
> God is greater, God is greater, God is truly greater. Praise be to God in abundance! Glory be to God early and late, there is no god but God, One, without partner, our *dīn* is wholly for Him though disbelievers may be averse. He has fulfilled His promise, given aid to His servant, alone defeated the clans. There is no god but God. God is greater.

Then he should offer the sacrifice (*hadyi*) if he has one with him. It is recommended that he do this himself, saying [as he makes the cut],

> بسم الله، والله أكبر، اللّٰهُمَّ منك، وبك، وإليك، تقبل مني، كما تقبلت من خليلك إبراهيم
>
> In the name of God, God is greater. O God, from You, in You, and to You. Accept from me [this sacrifice] as You accepted it from Your friend, Abraham.[83]

The best sacrifice to offer is a camel, next a cow, a goat, or a sheep. [For one person] to offer this is better than for six people to share a camel or cow, and a ram is better than a goat, following the saying of the Messenger ﷺ of God, "The best of all animals to sacrifice is a ram with horns,"[84] and of these, the white is preferred

---

83 In Abū Dāwūd, *Sunan*, 2795, it is related that the Prophet ﷺ sacrificed two excellent rams with horns. When he turned them in the direction of the prayer, he said, *Indeed, I have turned my face toward He who created the heavens and the earth* [Q. 6:79] and following the religion of Abraham, pure monotheism, *Say, Indeed, my prayer, my rites of sacrifice, my living and my dying are for God, Lord of the worlds. No partner has He. And this I have been commanded* ... [Q. 6:162–163] and I am one of the Muslims. O God, from You and for You, and for Muḥammad and his community. In the name of God, God is greater." Then he made the sacrifice.

84 Abū Dāwūd, *Sunan*, 3156; al-Tirmidhī, *Sunan*, 1517; Ibn Mājah, *Sunan*, 3130.

to the dust-colored or black, even as Abū Hurayra said, "A white [ram] is better to sacrifice than two black ones."[85]

If the sacrifice is made as a supererogatory act, then he should eat from it. He should not offer as a sacrifice animals that are lame, or have had their nose or ears cut, or are lacking horns, or are too small, or suffer from mange, or have had their ear split from above, or from below or have had their ears perforated in front, or from behind, or animals that are emaciated.

[A male pilgrim] should then shave [his head]. [According to] the *sunna* he should do this while facing the direction of prayer and begin from the forehead, and from the right side, all the way to the two bones at the nape of the neck, then shave the rest, saying,

> اللّٰهُمَّ، أثبت لي بكل شعرة حسنة، وامح عني بها سيئة، وارفع لي بها عندك درجة
> O God, for every hair shaved off, affirm for me a good deed, and efface from me a bad one, and raise my standing with You a degree.[86]

The female pilgrim should trim [her] hair and if a male pilgrim is bald, it is recommended that he only pass a razor over his head. With the act of shaving, after having thrown pebbles [at the first pillar], the pilgrim has completed the first stage of leaving *iḥrām*; this makes all the things he had to avoid while in *iḥrām* permissible for him except [for sexual contact] with women and hunting.

He then goes forth to Mecca and performs *ṭawāf* in the manner we have already described. This *ṭawāf* is a pillar (*rukn*) of the pilgrimage and is called the "*ṭawāf* of the visit."[87] The earliest time it can be done [starts] after midnight on the eve of the day of sacrifice, and the best time for it is on the day of sacrifice itself, but there is no end to its time. [The pilgrim] can delay it up to any time he wills, but he remains bound by *iḥrām*. This means that [sexual contact with] women is not lawful to him until he completes the *ṭawāf*.

---

85 ʿAbd al-Razzāq, *al-Muṣannaf*, 4:387; Ibn Ḥanbal, *Musnad*, 2:417; al-Ḥākim al-Nīsābūrī, *al-Mustadrak*, 4:227.

86 Al-Fākihī, *Akhbār Makka*, 1:190. The commentary adds that he should say the *takbīr* after completing this, he should bury his hair, and pray two cycles. And if he chooses just to shorten his hair, he should shorten all of it. See al-Zabīdī, *Itḥāf*, 4:399.

87 More commonly called *ṭawāf al-ifāḍa* (the circumambulation at the pouring forth).

When that happens, then he leaves *iḥrām* entirely and [everything] become permissible. At this point, his *iḥrām* is entirely removed and nothing remains to be done except casting pebbles during the days of *tashrīq*[88] and camping at Minā. These are duties after the *iḥrām* is lifted, in keeping with the rites of the pilgrimage.

The manner of [doing] this *ṭawāf* together with two cycles [of prayer] has been described [above] in the discussion of the *ṭawāf* of arrival. Then he finishes the two cycles, and the course [between Ṣafā and Marwā] as described above, if he did not already do so after the *ṭawāf* of arrival. If he has already done the *saʿī*, then that constitutes fulfilling a pillar [of the pilgrimage] and it is not necessary for him to repeat it.

He leaves *iḥrām* by three means: throwing the pebbles, shaving his head, and completing the essential *ṭawāf*. When he has completed two of these three, he attains the first stage of leaving *iḥrām*. There is no compulsion for the pilgrim to do either one before or after the sacrifice, but the most recommended order is to throw the pebbles [first], then make the sacrifice, then shave [his head], and then complete the *ṭawāf*.

On this day, it is *sunna* for the *imām* to deliver a sermon after the sun passes the meridian.[89] This is [in remembrance of] the farewell sermon of the Messenger صَلَّىٰ ٱللَّٰهُ عَلَيْهِ وَسَلَّمَ of God. Thus, there are four sermons during the pilgrimage. The first is the sermon on the seventh day [of Dhū l-Ḥijja], then the sermon on the day of ʿArafa, the sermon on the day of the sacrifice, and the sermon of the day of the first dispersal. Each of them is a single sermon with the exception of [the sermon on] the day of ʿArafa which is [delivered] in two parts, with a brief sitting in between.

When he [the pilgrim] finishes the *ṭawāf*, he returns to Minā in order to camp there and cast the pebbles. He spends that night at Minā, this being called the night of settling, because people also spend the next day at Minā and do not leave.

When the second day of the feast (*ʿīd*) arises and the sun has passed the meridian, the pilgrim should make the greater ablution

---

88 The three days following the day of sacrifice.

89 In this section Imām al-Ghazālī uses juristic and astronomical terminology; the reference to the meridian means past midday, after the start of noon (*ẓuhr*) prayer.

to cast the pebbles.[90] Then he should head to the first pillar, the one nearest ʿArafa, on the right of the principle road, and [he should] cast seven pebbles at it. When he has gone past it, he should go beyond it a little toward the right side of the road and then stand, turn in the direction of prayer, give praise to God تَعَالَىٰ, repeat the formula of oneness [*Lā ilāha illā Allāh*] and the *takbīr*, and supplicate God with presence of heart and physical reverence. He [the pilgrim] should stand facing the direction of prayer for the length of time it takes to recite Sūrat al-Baqara [Q. 2],[91] and concentrate on supplication.

Then he [should] proceed to the middle pillar, and cast [seven more] pebbles, as he did at the first, and afterward, stand on the road as he stood after the first.

Then he should proceed to the last pillar and throw seven [more pebbles]. Following this, he should not do anything or stop for supplications [as he did after the first two], but rather return to his campsite and spend that night at Minā. This night is called the night of the first dispersal.

He should stay until morning [at Minā] and then, when he has prayed the noon prayer (*ẓuhr*) on that second day of the days of *tashrīq*, he should throw twenty-one [more] pebbles, just as he did the day before. Then he can choose to stay at Minā or return to Mecca. If he leaves Minā before sunset, he is free to go, but if he is still there after sunset, then he should not leave, but rather spend the night [there] in order to again throw twenty-one more pebbles on that day, the day of the second dispersal, and throw them as he did the previous day.

A pilgrim who omits that night [at Minā] and throwing the pebbles on that day is required to make a sacrifice, and the meat of this sacrifice must be given in charity [to the poor].[92] The pilgrim is permitted to visit the sacred house [complex] during the nights of Minā, as long as he returns to sleep the night at Minā. This is what the Messenger صَلَّى ٱللَّٰهُ عَلَيْهِ وَسَلَّمَ of God used to do. He should not miss

---

90 As mentioned in Book 3 of the *Revival of the Religous Sciences: The Mysteries of Purification*, this is *sunna*, not obligatory.

91 This would be between forty-five minutes and one hour. However, the suggestion is not for the pilgrim to recite all of this *sūra*, but rather to try to stand in supplication and praise for that length of time.

92 That is, the pilgrim is not allowed to eat any of it.

[praying] the obligatory [prayers] with the *imām* in the mosque of al-Khayf, for there is great merit in doing so. When he goes forth from Minā, it is best for him to stay at al-Muḥaṣṣab,[93] adjacent to Minā, and [while he is] there pray afternoon (*ʿaṣr*), sunset (*maghrib*), and evening (*ʿishāʾ*) [prayers]. He should then have a short rest. This is a *sunna* reported by a number of the Companions رَضِيَٱللَّهُعَنْهُ, but there is no harm if he omits it.

Part 8: A Description of the Visit (*ʿUmra*) and What Follows It Up to the *Ṭawāf* of Farewell

WHOEVER intends [to perform] the visit, [whether] before his pilgrimage or after it, must make the greater ablution, wear the [two] cloths of *iḥrām* in the way previously mentioned for the pilgrimage, and enter *iḥrām* for the lesser pilgrimage at its [correct] station (*mīqāt*).

[For the visit], the best station is Jiʿrāna, then Tanʿīm, then al-Ḥudaybiyya.[94]

He [should] then make his intention to perform the visit and recites the *talbiyya*. He [should] go to the mosque of ʿĀʾisha رَضِيَٱللَّهُعَنْهَا and pray two cycles, and supplicate for whatever he wants, then return to Mecca reciting the *talbiyya* until he enters the sacred mosque. When he enters the mosque, he [should] cease the *talbiyya* and complete seven circumambulations (*ṭawāf*) around [the Kaʿba], followed by the seven laps [between Ṣafā and Marwā], all in the way that we have already described. When he finishes this, he [should] shave his head, and his visit is then complete.

For those who live in Mecca, it is recommended that they complete the visit and make *ṭawāf* frequently, and also that they look on the house [Kaʿba] often. If [a pilgrim] enters [the actual Kaʿba], he should pray two cycles between the two pillars,[95] for that

93 A valley between Minā and Mecca.

94 Jiʿrāna is about twelve miles from Mecca on the road to Taif. Tanʿīm, the closest, is a little more than four miles from Mecca, and al-Ḥudaybiyya, famous for the treaty that was signed there, is approximately nine miles from Mecca.

95 A *ḥadīth* in al-Bukhārī, *Ṣaḥīḥ*, 505, and elsewhere quotes ʿAbdallāh b. ʿUmar as saying that the Prophet صَلَّىٱللَّهُعَلَيْهِوَسَلَّمَ entered the Kaʿba with a number of the Companions

is most excellent. Indeed, if he enters [the Kaʿba itself], he should do so barefooted and in awe.

> Once one of [the pious] was asked, "Have you entered the house of your Lord today?"
>
> He said, by God, I do not see these two feet [of mine] worthy of even walking around the house of my Lord, so how could I see them as worthy of taking one step in the house of my Lord, when I know when they have walked and where?[96]

He should drink the water of Zamzam abundantly, drawing its water without help if possible, and he should quench his thirst and drink until he is entirely full.[97] Then he should say,

> اللّٰهُمَّ، اجعله شفاء من كل داء وسقم، وارزقني الإخلاص واليقين، والمعافاة في الدنيا والآخرة
>
> O God, make it a cure for every disease and sickness, and provide me with sincerity, certainty, and well-being in this world and the next.[98]

The Prophet ﷺ said, "The water of Zamzam is for whatever it is drunk." That is, it cures any ailment for which it is drunk.[99]

Part 9: On the *Ṭawāf* of Farewell

When it appears to [the pilgrim time] to return to his homeland after completing the pilgrimage and visit, he should first settle his affairs, ready his mount, and his final act is to the farewell to the house. His farewell is a [last] *ṭawāf* of seven circumambulations as

---

and spent some time inside. When they came out, ʿAbdallāh asked Bilāl what the Prophet ﷺ had done and the latter [Bilāl] responded, "He stood so that one pillar was on his left, one on his right, and three others behind him … and prayed." The version in Mālik, *al-Muwaṭṭaʾ* specifies, "two pillars on his right." At present, there are three pillars inside the Kaʿba.

96 Abū Nuʿaym, *Ḥilya*, 8:150.

97 *Taḍalluʿ* in this context means to drink so much that one's ribs (*aḍlāʿ*) stretch. This is mentioned in Ibn Mājah, *Sunan*, 3061.

98 ʿAbd al-Razzāq, *al-Muṣannaf*, 113; al-Dāraquṭnī, *Sunan*, 2:288, with similar wording.

99 Ibn Mājah, *Sunan*, 3062.

previously [described] but without trotting (*ramal*) and without his [pilgrim's] garb.

On completing [the *ṭawāf*], he should pray two cycles behind the station [of Abraham], drink from the water of Zamzam, then go to Multazim[100] and humbly supplicate God with these words:

اللَّهُمَّ، إن البيت بيتك، والعبد عبدك، وابن عبدك، وابن أمتك، حملتني على ما سخرت لي من خلقك، حتى سيرتني في بلادك، وبلغتني بنعمتك، حتى أعنتني على قضاء مناسكك، فإن كنت رضيت عني . . فازدد عني رضا، وإلا . . فمن الآن قبل تباعدي عن بيتك هذا أوان انصرافي إن أذنت لي غير مستبدل بك ولا ببيتك، ولا راغب عنك ولا عن بيتك، اللَّهُمَّ، أصحبني العافية في بدني، والعصمة في ديني، وأحسن منقلبي، وارزقني طاعتك أبدا ما أبقيتني، واجمع لي خير الدنيا والآخرة، إنك على كل شيء قدير، اللَّهُمَّ، لا تجعل هذا آخر عهدي ببيتك الحرام، وإن جعلته آخر عهدي . . فعوضني عنه الجنة

O God, this house is Your house and this servant is Your servant, the child of two of Your servants, a man and woman. You have borne me here on the creature You put under my control and thus brought me to Your land, and conveyed me by way of Your grace and helped me to complete the rites of the pilgrimage. If You have been content with me, add to Your contentment with me and if not, then bestow favor on me now, before I am far from Your house. This is my time to depart, if You permit me, but not for anything that takes Your place or the place of Your sacred house, nor for any desire to be distant from You or from Your sacred house. O God, grant that I go with well-being in my body, protection in my *dīn*, and a beautiful return. Provide me with obedience to You for as long as You keep me alive. Bring together for me the good of this world and the good of the hereafter. Verily, You have power over all things. O God, let this not be the end of my covenant [i.e., let this not be my last pilgrimage] with

100 Multazim is the small area between the [black] stone and the door of the Kaʿba (see fig. 2); al-Zabīdī, *Itḥāf*, 4:451.

> Your sacred house, but if You have made it so, then grant me heaven in its place.[101]

And it is preferred [lit. beloved] not to turn his eyes turn away from the house until he leaves it.

Part 10: On the Visit to Medina and the Conduct [of the Visitor]

The Messenger صَلَّى ٱللَّهُ عَلَيْهِ وَسَلَّمَ of God said, "To visit me after my death is like visiting me during my life."[102]

And he صَلَّى ٱللَّهُ عَلَيْهِ وَسَلَّمَ said, "Whoever finds wealth and does not come to me has neglected me."[103]

And he صَلَّى ٱللَّهُ عَلَيْهِ وَسَلَّمَ said, "If someone comes to me as a visitor with his only concern [being] to visit me, it is incumbent on God سُبْحَانَهُ that I be his intercessor."[104]

Whoever sets out to visit Medina should invoke blessings on the Messenger صَلَّى ٱللَّهُ عَلَيْهِ وَسَلَّمَ of God abundantly, [all] along the way.

Then, when he catches [the first] glimpse of its walls and its trees, he should say,

> اللّٰهُمَّ، هذا حرم رسولك، فاجعله لي وقاية من النار، وأمانا من العذاب، وسوء الحساب
>
> O God, this is the sanctuary of Your Messenger. Make it a protection for me from the fire and a safety from punishment and a bad reckoning.

He should perform the greater ablution before entering [the city] at the well of Ḥarra[105] and he should use scent and put on his best and cleanest clothes. When he enters it, he should enter with humility and veneration and he should say [at that moment],

101 Al-Bayhaqī, *al-Sunan al-kubrā*, 5:163.

102 Al-Ṭabarānī, *al-Muʿjam al-awsaṭ*, 289, 3400; al-Dāraquṭnī, *Sunan*, 2:278; al-Bayhaqī, *al-Sunan al-kubrā*, 5:246.

103 Ibn ʿAdī, *al-Kāmil*, 7:14.

104 Al-Ṭabarānī, *al-Muʿjam al-kabīr*, 12:291; Abū Nuʿaym, *Tārīkh Iṣbahān*, 2:190.

105 On the outskirts of town.

بسم الله، وعلى ملة رسول الله: رَّبِّ أَدْخِلْنِي مُدْخَلَ صِدْقٍ وَأَخْرِجْنِي مُخْرَجَ صِدْقٍ وَٱجْعَل لِّي مِن لَّدُنكَ سُلْطَٰنًا نَّصِيرًا ﴿٨٠﴾

"In the name of God and the religion (*milla*) of the Messenger ﷺ of God ... "*My Lord, cause me to enter a sound entrance and to exit a sound exit and grant me from Yourself a supporting authority* [17:80].

Then he should go to the mosque [of the Prophet], enter it, and pray two cycles next to the pulpit (*minbar*),[106] standing with the pillar of the *minbar* opposite his right shoulder and facing the column next to which is the box, with the circle indicating the direction of prayer for the mosque in front of him. That was the place where the Messenger ﷺ of God stood before the mosque was changed, so the visitor should try his best to offer the prayer [as though he were] in the original mosque before they expanded it.

Then he should go to the tomb of the Prophet ﷺ and stand near [the Prophet's] face. He [should] do this by turning his back to the direction of prayer and facing the wall of the tomb at [a distance of] about four arm spans from the pillar that stands in the corner of the wall of the tomb, with the candle-holder above his head. It is not part of the *sunna* to touch or kiss this wall. Rather, [he should] stand at a distance from it, [for that] is more respectful. He should stand, then say,

السلام عليك يا رسول الله، السلام عليك يا نبي الله، السلام عليك يا أمين الله، السلام عليك يا حبيب الله، السلام عليك يا صفوة الله، السلام عليك يا خيرة الله، السلام عليك يا أحمد، السلام السلام عليك يا محمد، السلام عليك يا أبا القاسم، السلام عليك يا ماحي، السلام عليك يا عاقب، السلام عليك يا حاشر، السلام عليك يا بشير، السلام عليك يا نذير، السلام عليك يا طهر، السلام عليك يا طاهر، السلام عليك يا أكرم ولد آدم، السلام عليك يا سيد المرسلين، السلام

106 The *minbar* is a staircase usually situated to the right of the prayer niche (*miḥrāb*) or *qibla* of a mosque; it may be rudimentary and mobile or ornate and built of stone and immobile. It is used to elevate the *imām* over the congregation in order that he may be seen and his sermon heard by all those who attend the Friday congregational prayer and the ʿ*īd* prayers.

عليك يا خاتم النبيين، السلام عليك يا رسول رب العالمين، السلام عليك يا قائد الخير، السلام عليك يا فاتح البر، السلام عليك يا نبي الرحمة، السلام عليك يا هادي الأمة، السلام عليك يا قائد الغر المحجلين

Peace be on you, O Messenger of God. Peace be on you, O Prophet of God. Peace be on you, O trusted one of God. Peace be on you, O beloved of God. Peace be on you, O chosen [one] of God. Peace be on you, O [most] excellent before God. Peace be on you, O Aḥmad. Peace be on you, O Muḥammad. Peace be on you, O Abū l-Qāsim. Peace be on you, [who] effaces [disbelief]. Peace be on you, [who] ends [the line of prophets]. Peace be on you, [who] gathers together. Peace be on you, [who] brings good news. Peace be on you, [who] warns of danger. Peace be on you, who is pure. Peace be on you, who purifies others. Peace be on you, O most generous of the children of Adam. Peace be on you, O leader of the messengers. Peace be on you, O seal of the prophets. Peace be on you, O Messenger of the Lord of the worlds. Peace be on you, who ordains toward goodness. Peace be on you, who is the opening to goodness. Peace be on you, O Prophet of mercy. Peace be on you, O guide to the community. Peace be on you, who will lead those illuminated by the ablution [on the day of judgment].

السلام عليك، وعلى أهل بيتك، الذين أذهب الله عنهم الرجس، وطهرهم تطهيرا

Peace be on you and on the people of your house (*ahl al-bayt*) whom God has cleansed of all impurities and made pure.

السلام عليك، وعلى أصحابك الطيبين، وعلى أزواجك الطاهرات، أمهات المؤمنين

Peace be on you and on your pure Companions and your wives, the pure mothers of believers.

جزاك الله عنا، أفضل ما جزى نبيا عن قومه، ورسولا عن أمته، وصلى عليك كلما ذكرك الذاكرون، وكلما غفل عنك الغافلون، وصلى عليك في الأولين والآخرين، أفضل وأكمل وأعلى وأجل، وأطيب وأطهر، ما صلى على أحد من خلقه، كما استنقذنا بك من الضلالة، وبصرنا بك من العماية، وهدانا بك من الجهالة

May God reward you on our behalf with the best reward ever bestowed on any prophet on behalf of his folk, or on any messenger on behalf of his community, and may He bless you with remembrance as often as those who remember you and as often as the neglectful forget to remember you. May God bless you among the first and the last, with the most excellent, the most generous, the most exalted, the grandest, the sweetest, and purest blessings ever granted to any one of His creatures—as He delivered us through you from being astray, and through you opened our eyes after blindness, and through you guided us from ignorance.

أشهد أن لا إله إلا الله، وحده لا شريك له، وأشهد أنك عبده ورسوله، وأمينه وصفيه، وخيرته من خلقه، وأشهد أنك قد بلغت الرسالة، وأديت الأمانة، ونصحت الأمة، وجاهدت عدوك وهديت أمتك، وعبدت ربك حتى أتاك اليقين، فصلى الله عليك، وعلى أهل بيتك الطيبين، وسلم وشرف وكرم وعظم

I testify that there is no god but God, alone, without partner, and I testify that you are His servant and His Messenger, His trusted one and His elect, and His chosen among His creatures. I testify that you delivered the message, fulfilled the trust, counseled the community, strove against your foes, guided your community, and worshiped your Lord until what is certain came to you.[107] May God send blessings on you and the sweet and pure people of your house, along with salutations of peace, nobility, honor, and esteem.

If the pilgrim was asked to convey the greetings of another, he should say, "Peace be on you from so-and-so, peace be on you from so-and so."

Then, he should move back one arm span and greet Abū Bakr al-Ṣiddīq رَضِيَ ٱللَّهُ عَنْهُ, for his head lies by the shoulder of the Messenger صَلَّى ٱللَّهُ عَلَيْهِ وَسَلَّمَ of God, while the head of ʿUmar رَضِيَ ٱللَّهُ عَنْهُ lies by the shoulder of Abū Bakr رَضِيَ ٱللَّهُ عَنْهُ. Then, he should step back one

107 This prayer echoes the Qurʾān: *So exalt* [*God*] *with praise of your Lord and be of those who prostrate* [*to Him*]. *And worship your Lord until there comes to you the certainty* [*death*] [15:98–99].

more arm span and greet al-Fārūq ʿUmar رَضِيَ ٱللَّهُ عَنْهُ and say [addressing both him and Abū Bakr],

> السلام عليكما، يا وزيري رسول الله صَلَّى ٱللَّهُ عَلَيْهِ وَسَلَّمَ، والمعاونين له على القيام بالدين ما دام حيا، والقائمين في أمته بعده بأمور الدين، تتبعان في ذلك آثاره، وتعملان بسنته، فجزاكما الله خير ما جزى وزيري نبي عن دينه
>
> Peace be on you both, O helpers of the Messenger صَلَّى ٱللَّهُ عَلَيْهِ وَسَلَّمَ of God. You helped him to establish the *dīn* as long as he was alive and took on the matters of *dīn* for his community, following in his footsteps and practicing his *sunna*. May God reward you [with] the best reward of any of those who helped a prophet in *dīn*.

Then he should return and stand beside the head of the Messenger صَلَّى ٱللَّهُ عَلَيْهِ وَسَلَّمَ of God, in the place that is nowadays between the tomb and the column, and turning in the direction of prayer, he should praise and glorify God عَزَّ وَجَلَّ and invoke many blessings on the Messenger صَلَّى ٱللَّهُ عَلَيْهِ وَسَلَّمَ of God. Then he should say,

> اللّٰهُمَّ إنك قد قلت وقولك الحق، وَلَوْ أَنَّهُمْ إِذ ظَّلَمُوٓاْ أَنفُسَهُمْ جَآءُوكَ فَٱسْتَغْفَرُواْ ٱللَّهَ وَٱسْتَغْفَرَ لَهُمُ ٱلرَّسُولُ لَوَجَدُواْ ٱللَّهَ تَوَّابًا رَّحِيمًا، اللّٰهُمَّ إنا قد سمعنا قولك، وأطعنا أمرك، وقصدنا نبيك، متشفعين به إليك في ذنوبنا، وما أثقل ظهورنا من أوزارنا، تائبين من زللنا معترفين بخطايانا وتقصيرنا، فتب اللّٰهُمَّ علينا، وشفع نبيك هذا فينا، وارفعنا بمنزلته عندك وحقه عليك، اللّٰهُمَّ اغفر للمهاجرين والأنصار، واغفر لنا ولإخواننا الذين سبقونا بالأيمان، اللّٰهُمَّ لا تجعله آخر العهد من قبر نبيك، ومن حرمك، يا أرحم الراحمين
>
> "O God! You have said—and Your word is true—*And if, when they had wronged themselves, they had but come to you and asked forgiveness of God, and asked forgiveness of the Messenger, they would have found God the All-Forgiving and Most-Merciful* [4:64] O God! We have heard Your words and have obeyed Your command and have come here to Your Prophet seeking intercession through him before You for our sins and the burdens that weigh heavily on us [lit. our backs], turning in repentance for our faults, confessing our transgressions

and shortcomings. O God! Accept our repentance and let this, Your Prophet, intercede for us, and elevate us by virtue of his place and his merit before You. O God! Forgive the Emigrants (Muhājirīn) and the Helpers (Anṣār), forgive us and our brothers who preceded us in the faith. O God! Do not make this our final covenant with the tomb of Your Prophet and with Your sanctuary, O Most Merciful of the merciful."

Then he should go to the inner garden (*rawḍa*) and pray two cycles, followed by as many supplications as he is able, for the Prophet ﷺ said, "Between my tomb and my *minbar* is a garden from among the gardens of heaven, and my *minbar* stands on my pool."[108]

He should make supplications near the *minbar* and it is recommended that he place his hand on the lowest post [of the bannister], for this is where the Messenger ﷺ of God placed his hand while he delivered sermons.[109]

On Thursday it is commendable to go to Uḥud to visit the tombs of the martyrs, and offer the *fajr* prayer in the mosque of the Prophet ﷺ of God. He should set out and return again to offer the *ẓuhr* prayer in the mosque so that no obligatory prayer is missed in the congregation in the mosque of the Messenger ﷺ of God.

It is also recommended that he set out every day to Baqīʿ and after greeting the Messenger ﷺ of God visit the tomb of ʿUthmān رضي الله عنه and Ḥasan b. ʿAlī رضي الله عنهما. The tombs of ʿAlī b. al-Ḥusayn, Muḥammad b. ʿAlī, and Jaʿfar b. Muḥammad رضي الله عنهم are also there. He should also offer the prayer in the mosque[110] of Fāṭima رضي الله عنها and visit the tomb of Ibrāhīm, the son of the Messenger ﷺ of God, and Ṣafiyya, the aunt of the Messenger ﷺ of God. All this is in al-Baqīʿ.

It is recommended that the pilgrim go to the mosque of Qubāʾ every Saturday and pray there, for it is reported that the Messenger ﷺ

108 Al-Bukhārī, *Ṣaḥīḥ*, 1196; Muslim, *Ṣaḥīḥ*, 1391.

109 The commentary points out that in 654/1256 (after al-Ghazālī's time), a fire struck the Prophet's mosque and the *minbar* was completely changed. Al-Zabīdī, *Ithāf*, 4:422.

110 In al-Ghazālī's time, the mosque of Fāṭima was in Baqīʿ, but it is no longer there.

of God said, "Whoever leaves his house, goes to the mosque of Qubāʾ, and prays there has done what is equal to the visit (ʿ*umra*)."[111]

It is recommended [that the pilgrim] visit the well of Arīs. It is said that the Prophet ﷺ spat into it for the purpose of curing. This well is by the mosque,[112] and the pilgrim should perform the ablution with [its water] and drink from it. He should also go to al-Fatḥ Mosque which lies on the trench[113] and the rest of the mosques and shrines as well.

It is said that in Medina there are a total of thirty mosques and shrines that the local people know. So [the pilgrim] should set out [to visit] as many as he can, [and the same is true] for the wells where the Messenger ﷺ of God performed the ablution. He should wash and drink from the latter—and these number seven—seeking the healing property of their waters and the blessings that come [from drinking from them].

If it is possible for him to stay [for some time] in Medina and observe its sanctity, there is great merit in this, for the Prophet ﷺ said, "There is no one who endures the hardships and severity of Medina except that I will be his intercessor on the day of judgment."[114] And also, "Anyone who is able to die in Medina should do so, for no one dies there except that I will be his intercessor on the day of resurrection."[115]

When he has finished all his affairs in Medina and intends to depart, it is recommended that he go once more to the noble tomb and repeat the supplications of the visit, as has been described, then bid farewell to the Messenger ﷺ of God, and ask that God عَزَّوَجَلَّ might provide him with a chance to return, and safety on his journey [home]. Then he should pray two cycles in the small *rawḍa*, this being the place where the Messenger ﷺ of God stood before the enclosure (*maqṣūra*) of the mosque was

111 Al-Nasāʾī, *Sunan*, 2:37; Ibn Mājah, *Sunan*, 1412.

112 That is, Qubāʾ Mosque.

113 The battle of the trench in 5/627 took place at this location.

114 Muslim, *Ṣaḥīḥ*, 1363.

115 Al-Tirmidhī, *Sunan*, 3917; Ibn Mājah, *Sunan*, 3112.

added.[116] When he leaves the mosque, he should put his left foot outside the mosque first, then his right, and say,

> اللّٰهُمَّ، صل على محمد، وعلى آل محمد، ولا تجعله آخر العهد بنبيك، وحط أوزاري بزيارته، وأصحبني في سفري السلامة، ويسر رجوعي إلى أهلي ووطني سالما، يا ارحم الراحمين
> O God, send blessings on Muḥammad and on the family of Muḥammad, and let this not be [my] last visit with Your Prophet. Remove the burden of my sins by this visit to him, let me go on my journey in peace, and return me to my family and homeland with ease and safety, O Most Merciful of the merciful.

He should also give what he can in charity to those who live as neighbors to the Messenger ﷺ of God and follow the mosques, which number twenty, that lie between Medina and Mecca and pray in each of them.

A Section on the *Sunna* of Returning from a Journey

THE Messenger ﷺ of God, on returning from a battle or from the pilgrimage or any other [longer] journey, would repeat the *takbīr* [*Allāhu Akbar*] three times when climbing any ridge to higher ground. He would [also] say,

> لا إله إلا الله، وحده لا شريك له، له الملك، وله الحمد، وهو على كل شيء قدير، آيبون تائبون عابدون ساجدون لربنا حامدون، صدق الله وعده، ونصر عبده ،وهزم الأحزاب وحده) وفي بعض الروايات (وكل شيء هالك إلا وجهه، له الحكم وإليه ترجعون)
> There is no god except God, alone, without partner. The kingdom and the praise is for Him, and He has power over all things. We return seeking repentance, worshiping, prostrating to our Lord and praising [Him]. God has kept His promise, has given aid to His servant, and He alone has defeated the

116 The *maqṣūra* refers to an enclosure near the prayer niche that was later added to some of the larger mosques. Its purpose was to protect the ruler as he was standing in prayer. See Book 4 of the *Revival of the Religous Sciences: The Mysteries of the Prayer*, 108 n.68.

> clans.[117] (In some versions of this invocation, these words are added:) All things perish except His countenance. The rule is His and to Him you return.[118]

This is the *sunna* the pilgrim should follow on his return.

When he comes into view of his hometown, he should hasten the pace of the animal [he is riding] and say,

اللّٰهُمَّ، اجعل لنا بها قراراً ورزقاً حسنا

> O God, make a place for us to dwell [in peace] there and a goodly provision.[119]

Then he should send someone to his family to inform them of his arrival so as not to reach home unexpectedly. This is the *sunna*. In fact, he should not knock on [the door of] his home at night.[120] When he enters the town, he should go to the mosque to pray two cycles, for this is a *sunna* and this is what the Messenger ﷺ of God used to do.

When [the pilgrim] enters his house, he should do so [while] saying,

توباً توباً لربنا أوباً لا يغادر علينا حوباً

> Repenting, repenting, to our Lord returning, may He leave not one of our sins unforgiven.[121]

And when he is settled back in his house, he should not forget the blessings that God gave him—the visit to His house, His sanctuary, and the tomb of His Prophet ﷺ—[and he should not] be ungrateful for that blessing and return to a state of heedlessness, distraction, and occupation with sin. For that [to happen] is not a sign of an accepted pilgrimage. Rather, its sign [of acceptance] is for him to return in a state of withdrawal from this world, with renewed aspiration toward the hereafter, and readiness, after having met the house of the Lord, to meet the Lord of the house.

---

117 Al-Bukhārī, *Ṣaḥīḥ*, 1797; Muslim, *Ṣaḥīḥ*, 1344.

118 Al-Maḥāmilī, *al-Duʿāʾ*, 77.

119 Al-Maḥāmilī, *al-Duʿāʾ*, 95.

120 By which he means after the *ʿishāʾ* prayer.

121 Ibn Ḥanbal, *Musnad*, 1:255.

3

On the Detailed Rules of Conduct and Inward Practices

Ten Detailed Rules of Conduct [in Respect to the Pilgrimage]

[Expenditures]

FIRST, everything the pilgrim spends [for the pilgrimage] must be lawfully earned and [his] hands [must] be free of any business that will distract [his] heart and mind; his sole concern should be God تَعَالَىٰ, so [his] heart will be at peace, directed toward the remembrance of God تَعَالَىٰ and the veneration of His sacred sites.

It has been reported by [members of the Prophet's] household: "When the end of time draws near, people will go on the pilgrimage in four [different groups]. The rulers will go as an excursion, the rich will go on business, the poor will go to beg, and the [Qurʾān] reciters will go to become famous."[1]

This tradition sums up all the worldly reasons which can be imagined in relation to the pilgrimage and all of these prevent [a pilgrim] from [attaining] the merit of the pilgrimage, and keep him from [reaching] the realm of the pilgrimage of the elect. This is especially true for [someone] performing it solely on behalf of someone else and for a fee. In doing this, he is seeking this world through a practice of the hereafter. All those with scruples, all the

1 Al-Khaṭīb al-Baghdādī, *Tārīkh Baghdād*, 10:295, with similar wording.

people of the heart, have disapproved of these actions [mentioned in the report], unless the pilgrim intends to reside in Mecca and has no other means to get there. If such be his purpose, then there is no harm in his receiving [remuneration to make the pilgrimage for another], for he is not using *dīn* as a means to gain the world, but rather using the world as a means to the *dīn*. In this, his aim should be to visit the house of God عَزَّوَجَلَّ and to help his Muslim brother fulfill his obligation. It is in respect to such a case that the Messenger صَلَّىٱللَّهُعَلَيْهِوَسَلَّمَ of God said, "God سُبْحَانَهُ, will bring three people into heaven for a single pilgrimage: the one who bequeaths [wealth to perform it], the one who executes a will, and the one who performs it on behalf of his brother."

I am not saying that the fee is unlawful or that it is unlawful for him to do this if he has fulfilled the obligation [of pilgrimage] for himself. But it is better not to do it, and not to adopt this as his way of earning money and trade, for God عَزَّوَجَلَّ may give the world by way of *dīn* but not *dīn* by way of the world. Thus, in a tradition it is stated: "The example of one who fights in a battle of the sake of God عَزَّوَجَلَّ and then receives compensation for it is like the example of the mother of Moses عَلَيْهِٱلسَّلَامُ who nursed her own child and was paid for it."[2]

If someone is in a situation analogous to the mother of Moses, [that is,] he is taking payment for the pilgrimage, there is no harm in it, for he is doing so in order that he himself may accomplish the pilgrimage and the visit. He is not performing the pilgrimage in order to receive payment, but rather receiving payment in order to perform the pilgrimage, as Moses' mother was paid to enable her to nurse [her own baby] while keeping her true situation hidden.

[Taxes]

Second, [the pilgrim] should not help the enemies of God, be He glorified, by paying them a tax[3] along the way. [These enemies] are the princes of Mecca and certain Bedouins who hinder people from the sacred mosque. To give them money [as tax] is helping them in

---

2 Ibn Abī Shayba, *al-Muṣannaf*, 19881; Abū Dāwūd, *al-Murāsil*, 318.

3 The *maks* seems to have been a kind of tax or toll collected from pilgrims along certain routes.

their wrongdoing and facilitating their means, which is tantamount to giving them personal help.

[The pilgrim] should kindly seek to avoid [paying this tax], but if he cannot, then one of the scholars has said (and I find no fault in his statement), "It is better to give up all supererogatory acts of pilgrimage and turn back than to assist transgressors). This is an [erroneous] innovation that has been instituted, and in yielding to it one helps make it a permanent custom. Moreover, it is belittling and degrading for the Muslims to pay such a tax.

There is no justification for someone's saying, "This was taken from me by force," for if he had stayed at home or turned back, nothing would have been taken from him. Rather, perhaps he showed [them that] he had the means to pay such a tax and so even more was sought from him, but if he had been dressed like the poor, nothing would have been asked. He is the one who put himself in the position of being forced to give.

[Provisions]

Third, the pilgrim should have enough provisions and a generous enough disposition to be able to spend [on himself and others] without stinginess or extravagance, but with frugality. By extravagance (*isrāf*) I mean enjoying a wide variety of foods, and indulging in the choicest of them, [as is] the habit of the affluent. However, with regard to being generous in giving in charity, this is not extravagance. "There is no goodness in extravagance and no extravagance in goodness," as someone said.[4] Giving charity from one's provision on the road to pilgrimage is spending for the sake of God عَزَّوَجَلَّ and one dirham [spent in this way] has the value of seven hundred dirhams [spent otherwise]. Ibn ʿUmar رَضِيَ ٱللَّهُ عَنْهُمَا said, "Part of the nobility of a man is to have good and abundant provision on his journey."[5] And he said, "The best pilgrim is the one who is most sincere in his intention, purest in what he spends, and best in certitude."[6]

4 A saying attributed to Ḥasan b. Sahl by Ibn ʿAbd al-Barr in *Bahjat al-majālis*, 2:614.

5 Abū Ṭālib al-Makkī, *Qūt al-qulūb*, 2:115.

6 Abū Ṭālib al-Makkī, *Qūt al-qulūb*, 2:115.

And the Prophet صَلَّى ٱللَّٰهُ عَلَيْهِ وَسَلَّمَ said, "An accepted pilgrimage has no recompense other than heaven"[7] and when he was asked, "O Messenger of God, what makes a pilgrimage accepted?" He answered, "Pure and wholesome speech and giving food [to the needy]."[8]

[Behavior]

Fourth, the [pilgrim] must cease all crudeness, immorality, and quarreling, as the Qurʾān commands.

"Obscenity" (*rafath*) is a noun that combines, in its meaning, all loose, indecent, and obscene talk. This includes saying anything amorous or provocative to women or flirting with them or speaking about sexual intercourse and what leads up to it, for all this excites the desire for sexual intercourse, which is forbidden. Whatever attracts [someone] to something forbidden is itself forbidden.

"Immorality" (*fusūq*) is a comprehensive term for everything that takes [one] away from obedience to God عَزَّوَجَلَّ.

"Quarreling" (*jidāl*) means excessively arguing over something, such that it provokes rancor, disperses one's aspiration, and breaches good conduct.

Sufyān al-Thawrī said, "Whoever uses obscene talk has ruined his pilgrimage."[9] And the Messenger صَلَّى ٱللَّٰهُ عَلَيْهِ وَسَلَّمَ of God made wholesome talk, along with feeding [the needy], a [sign] of a pilgrimage that has been accepted. Arguing annuls wholesome speech, so the pilgrim should avoid being at odds with his traveling companion, or camel driver, or other companions. Rather, he should incline toward them and "lower his wing"[10] to all other travelers to the house of God عَزَّوَجَلَّ.

He should maintain good character (*ḥusna al-khuluq*); good character does not mean simply refraining from hurting others, but also bearing the hurt [that may come from others]. It has been said that a "journey" is called *safar* because it "unveils" (*yusfiru*) men's character. For this reason ʿUmar رَضِيَ ٱللَّٰهُ عَنْهُ said to someone who claimed to know a [certain man], "Did you go with him on a journey that

---

7 Al-Bukhārī, *Ṣaḥīḥ*, 1773; Muslim, *Ṣaḥīḥ*, 1349, beginning with the words, "From visit (*ʿumra*) to visit is expiation for the sins that are committed between them..."

8 The phrase is found in Ibn Ḥanbal, *Musnad*, 3:325.

9 Abū Ṭālib al-Makkī, *Qūt al-qulūb*, 2:115.

10 This phrase echoes the Qurʾānic injunction, *And lower to them the wing of humility out of mercy* [17:24].

proved the nobility of his character?" "No," said the man. ʿUmar replied, "Then I do not think that you really know him."[11]

[Modes of Travel]

Fifth, he [should] perform the pilgrimage on foot if he can, for that is best. On his deathbed, ʿAbdallāh b. ʿAbbās رَضِيَ ٱللَّهُ عَنْهُمَا counseled his children with these words: "O my children, perform the pilgrimage on foot. For pilgrims on foot, every step he takes brings seven hundred good deeds done in the sanctuary." And when they asked him what that meant, he said, "One such deed is equal to one hundred thousand [done elsewhere]."[12]

The recommendation to walk while completing the actual rites of pilgrimage and when journeying from Mecca to the place of standing [at ʿArafa] and to Minā is more confirmed than [that of walking] on the way [to Mecca].

If, in addition to walking, the pilgrim dons the *iḥrām* from his family home, then that is said to be among the signs of making the pilgrimage complete, and ʿUmar, ʿAlī, and Ibn Masʿūd رَضِيَ ٱللَّهُ عَنْهُمْ all considered this to be the meaning of the words of God تَعَالَىٰ,

وَأَتِمُّوا۟ ٱلْحَجَّ وَٱلْعُمْرَةَ لِلَّهِ ۚ

And complete the ḥajj and ʿumra for God [2:196].

Some scholars, however, say that riding is better, because of what is spent for [the mount] and the supplies, and also because the pilgrim is less likely to become frustrated or injured, and more likely to preserve his health and safety and thus complete his pilgrimage.

On inspection, however, the latter view does not contradict the former [view, that he should walk from home]. Rather, it is better to be more specific and say that walking is better for one who finds it easy, but if it weakens him and leads him to have a bad disposition and fall short in his practice, then riding is better for him, just as fasting is better for a traveler or sick person, as long as it does not worsen his illness or give him a bad disposition.

---

11 Ibn Abī l-Dunyā, *al-Ṣamt wa-ādāb al-lisān*, 607.

12 Al-Ṭabarānī, *al-Muʿjam al-awsaṭ*, 2696; al-Ḥākim al-Nīsābūrī, *al-Mustadrak*, 1:460.

One of the scholars was asked about the visit (*ʿumra*), and whether it was best done walking or whether one should rent a donkey instead. He answered, "If the weight of the dirham [he will pay to rent the] donkey weighs more heavily [on his ego] than walking, then it is better for him to rent the donkey, but if walking is harder [on his ego]—as might be the case for a wealthy person—then it is better for him to walk."[13]

It is as if he [the scholar] responded from the point of view of striving against the ego, and there is some merit in this. However, it is better for the pilgrim to walk and spend that dirham on a good cause rather than giving it to a donkey driver in return for upsetting an animal. But if the [pilgrim's] ego is not broad enough to encompass both hardship and a decrease in wealth, then what the scholar said is not far from the truth.

[Conveyances]

Sixth, a pilgrim should not ride on anything other than a pack animal. He should avoid riding in a litter (*maḥmil*) unless he is afraid that he cannot keep himself on the pack animal. Riding in a litter should be avoided for two reasons: First, to make the burden lighter for the camel, for carrying a litter is hard on the camel; second to avoid the appearance of affluence and pride.

The Messenger ﷺ of God completed the pilgrimage riding a camel with a worn-out saddle and ragged blanket worth only four dirhams, and he made *ṭawāf* like this to show people his way and his all-inclusive character, and then he ﷺ said to them, "Learn your rites from me."[14]

It is said that these litters were innovated by al-Ḥajjāj, and that the scholars of his time rejected them.

Thus, it is related that Sufyān al-Thawrī conveyed that his father said, "I left Kūfa for al-Qādisiyya [on my way] to the pilgrimage and met up with people from other countries, and I saw that all the pilgrims were on pack animals with woven bags and laden camels, and I did not see one of them without a litter."[15]

13 Abū Ṭālib al-Makkī, *Qūt al-qulūb*, 2:117.

14 Muslim, *Ṣaḥīḥ*, 1297.

15 Abū Ṭālib al-Makkī, *Qūt al-qulūb*, 2:116.

Whenever he saw the drapes and litters that were innovated by al-Ḥajjāj, Ibn ʿUmar would say, "Though the caravan be great, the pilgrims are few." Then he looked at a poor man dressed in shabby clothes with only a saddle bag under him and said, "Here is one of the best of the pilgrims!"[16]

[Outward Appearance]

Seventh, the pilgrim should be shabby, disheveled, and dusty, and should not [seek to display] adornment or signs of pride and abundance. For [if he does] he will be reckoned among the haughty and well-off, and excluded from the company of the weak, the poor, and the elect of the pious. In a *ḥadīth* attributed to Faḍāla b. ʿUbayd, the Prophet ﷺ enjoined people to be disheveled and barefoot, and forbade luxury and opulence.[17]

Another *ḥadīth* [states]: "The pilgrim is uncombed and unadorned."[18] God تَعَالَىٰ says, "Look at those who come to visit My house. They come to Me unkempt and dusty from every narrow ravine."[19]

And He says,

ثُمَّ لْيَقْضُوا۟ تَفَثَهُمْ

Then let them end their untidiness [22:29].

Tafatha here means "being disheveled and dusty," while "to bring it to an end" (*yaqḍū*) means, "by shaving [their heads] and trimming their moustaches and fingernails."[20]

ʿUmar b. al-Khaṭṭāb رَضِيَ ٱللَّٰهُ عَنْهُ wrote to the commanders of the army, [saying], "Wear worn-out clothes and let your food be coarse."[21] And it has been said that the most beautiful of pilgrims are those from

16 Abū Ṭālib al-Makkī, *Qūt al-qulūb*, 2:116.

17 Abū Dāwūd, *Sunan*, 4160. This refers to not dressing ostentatiously and wearing clothes that are not conducive to self-conceit and pride.

18 Al-Tirmidhī, *Sunan*, 2998; Ibn Mājah, *Sunan*, 2896.

19 Al-Ṭabarānī, *al-Muʿjam al-kabīr*, 12:425; Abū Nuʿaym, *Ḥilya*, 3:305; al-Ḥākim al-Nīsābūrī, *al-Mustadrak*, 2:465 (without the last phrase); Ibn Ḥanbal, *Musnad*, 2:224.

20 Abū Ṭālib al-Makkī, *Qūt al-qulūb*, 2:116.

21 Al-Ḥarbī, *Gharīb al-ḥadīth*.

Yemen because they have a look of humility and weakness and thus preserve the way of the early believers.[22]

In particular, the pilgrim should avoid the color red in his clothing and any form of ostentation in general. It has been recorded that the Prophet صَلَّى ٱللَّهُ عَلَيْهِ وَسَلَّمَ was once on a journey and he and his Companions stopped to rest while the camels grazed. [It was then] that the Prophet صَلَّى ٱللَّهُ عَلَيْهِ وَسَلَّمَ saw red cloths on the pack-saddles and said, "I see this color red is predominant!" [One of the Companions said,] "On hearing this, we got up, went over to the camels, and pulled the [red] cloths off their backs [so quickly] that some of them became startled."[23]

[Treatment of Animals]

Eighth, the pilgrim should treat his mount with kindness. He should not load it with more than it has the strength to bear. A litter goes beyond the limits of its strength, while sleeping mounted on a camel can hurt the animal. People with scruples do not sleep while riding, other than to doze off a little while seated, nor do they remain mounted for a long time. The Prophet صَلَّى ٱللَّهُ عَلَيْهِ وَسَلَّمَ said, "Do not use the backs of your beasts as chairs."[24]

It is recommended that the pilgrim get off his mount every morning and evening to let it rest. This, in fact, is a *sunna*[25] and there are narratives about the early believers doing likewise. One of them would rent a mount with the understanding that he would not dismount and pay extra for that, but in fact, [they] would then dismount as an act of kindness to the animal and [in hopes] that it might be recorded among his good deeds and placed in his scale, not in the scale of the one who rented [his camel].[26]

Indeed, anyone who harms an animal and overloads it will pay for it on the day of judgment. Abū l-Dardāʾ said to his camel when it was dying, "O you, my camel, do not be my adversary before your Lord, for I have never loaded you with more than you could bear."[27]

---

22 Al-Ṭabarānī, *al-Muʿjam al-awsaṭ*, 3885.

23 Abū Dāwūd, *Sunan*, 4070.

24 Ibn Ḥanbal, *Musnad*, 3:441; al-Ḥākim al-Nīsābūrī, *al-Mustadrak*, 1:444.

25 Al-Bayhaqī, *al-Sunan al-kubrā*, 5:255.

26 Abū Ṭālib al-Makkī, *Qūt al-qulūb*, 2:116.

27 Ibn al-Mubārak, *Zuhd*, 1173. He notes that the camel's name was Damūn.

In sum, there is reward in doing good for any living creature, so the pilgrim should respect the rights of the animal and the rights of the one who rents it. If he dismounts from time to time, it gives the animal a rest and brings happiness to the heart of the one who rents it [to him]. A man once said to Ibn al-Mubārak, "Could you please carry this letter with you and deliver it to its destination?" He answered, "[Wait] until I ask permission from the owner, for I am only renting [the animal]."[28]

See, then, how scrupulous he was about taking with him a letter without weight. Such is the safest way with scruples, for if a door is opened to something small, little by little it will be opened to something large.

[Sacrifice]

Ninth, [the pilgrim] should approach God by making a sacrifice, even if this is not obligatory on him. He should make an effort to sacrifice one of the fattest and most costly livestock, and he should eat from it [as well as give it in charity], since it is supererogatory. If it were obligatory, he would not be permitted to eat any of it.

It is said that the saying of God تَعَالَىٰ,

ذَٰلِكَۖ وَمَن يُعَظِّمْ شَعَٰٓئِرَ ٱللَّهِ

That [*is so*]. *And whoever honors the symbols of God* [22:32]

refers to "making sure the sacrifice is goodly and fat."

To lead the sacrificial animal from the station of *iḥrām* is considered best, unless it would cause the animal hardship and suffering. The pilgrim should avoid bargaining for the animal, for the early believers used to pay a high price [for them], and disapproved of bargaining for three things: [an animal offered as] obligatory expiation, [an animal offered as a supererogatory] sacrifice, or the price of freeing a slave. In these, it is best for the price to be higher and more costly for the one paying it.

It was related by Ibn ʿUmar that ʿUmar رَضِيَ ٱللَّهُ عَنْهُ intended to offer a she-camel as expiation and the price asked was three hundred dinars. He asked the Messenger صَلَّى ٱللَّهُ عَلَيْهِ وَسَلَّمَ of God if he could buy it and

28 Abū Ṭālib al-Makkī, *Qūt al-qulūb*, 2:116.

then resell it in order to buy goats for its price and he ﷺ prohibited him from doing this, saying "Sacrifice [the she-camel] as the offering."[29] Because a little of something of high quality is better than a lot of something of low quality. Three hundred dinars is the price of thirty goats, and that is a lot of meat, but it is not [the quantity of] meat that is object, but rather the purification of the soul and cleansing it from avarice, and sacrificing a camel is greater before God عَزَّوَجَلَّ for

لَن يَنَالَ ٱللَّهَ لُحُومُهَا وَلَا دِمَآؤُهَا وَلَٰكِن يَنَالُهُ ٱلتَّقْوَىٰ مِنكُمْ

Their meat will not reach God, nor will their blood, but what reaches Him is piety from you [22:37]

and this can be achieved by insuring that what you offer is something precious in value regardless of its quantity.

The Messenger ﷺ of God was asked, "What is the goodness of the pilgrimage?" He answered "In ʿ*ajj* and *thajj*."[30] ʿ*Ajj* means raising the voice when chanting the *talbiyya* and *thajj* means making the sacrifice.

And ʿĀʾisha رَضِيَ ٱللَّهُ عَنْهَا reported that the Messenger ﷺ of God said, "On the day of the sacrifice no person can do anything more beloved to God عَزَّوَجَلَّ than to shed the blood [of the sacrificial animal], for [that animal] will be brought to the day of judgment with its horns and hoofs, and the blood that is spilt [is reckoned] by God عَزَّوَجَلَّ even before it falls to the earth." [ʿĀʾisha رَضِيَ ٱللَّهُ عَنْهَا added], "Therefore, be pleased to do it."[31]

A tradition also states "For every [piece of] wool on its skin a good deed [is written] for you, and for every drop of its blood, a good deed [is written]. All will be put in the scale, so rejoice."[32]

And the Prophet ﷺ said, "Choose your sacrificial animals with care, for they will be your mounts on the day of judgment."[33]

---

29 Abū Dāwūd, *Sunan*, 1756.

30 Al-Tirmidhī, *Sunan*, 827; Ibn Mājah, *Sunan*, 2896.

31 Al-Tirmidhī, *Sunan*, 1493; Ibn Mājah, *Sunan*, 3126.

32 Abū Ṭālib al-Makkī, *Qūt al-qulūb*, 2:118, with similar wording in Ibn Mājah, *Sunan*, 3127; al-Bayhaqī, *al-Sunan al-kubrā*, 9:283.

33 Al-Daylamī, *Musnad al-firdaws*, 268, with slightly different wording.

[Disposition]

Tenth, [the pilgrim] should maintain a good disposition with regard to what he spends for the sacrifice or with regard to any loss or affliction that might befall him, his possessions, or his body. Indeed, if a difficulty befalls him, it is proof that his pilgrimage is accepted, for to undergo difficulty in completing the pilgrimage is equal to spending for the sake of God تَعَالَىٰ: every dirham thus spent is equal to seven hundred [spent otherwise]. It is like the hardships undergone in battle for the sake of God, for every injury he endures and for every loss that afflicts him, there is reward, and so with God تَعَالَىٰ, he loses nothing.

Among the other signs that [his] pilgrimage has been accepted, it has been said that [the pilgrim] abandons the transgressions he used to commit and exchanges sinful companions for righteous ones, and [exchanges] gatherings of entertainment and neglect for gatherings of invocation and vigilance.[34]

An Explanation of the Inner Practices, of Sincere Intention, and of the Lessons To Be Received from Each of the Sacred Sites and How to Reflect on Them, with Mention of their Mysteries and Meanings, from the Beginning of the Pilgrimage to Its End

KNOW that the beginning of the pilgrimage is understanding, by which I mean an understanding of its place in *dīn*. Following this, there is the yearning to make it; the resolve to do so; the severing of attachments that hold one back; the purchase of the two cloths to be worn for the *iḥrām*; the purchase of provisions for the journey; the renting of a mount; the actual departure; the journey through the wilderness; entering the state of *iḥrām* at the stations, along with reciting the *talbiyya*; the entry into Mecca; and finally the completion of the rites as described above.

In each one of these steps there is a reminder to the one who will be reminded, a lesson for one to learn, an exhortation for every

34 Abū Ṭālib al-Makkī, *Qūt al-qulūb*, 2:119.

sincere aspirant, and an instruction and indication for the wise. Therefore, let us indicate the keys to each, so that when the door is opened to them, and their causes are known, some of their mysteries will be disclosed to each pilgrim in proportion to the clarity of his heart, his inner purity, and his deep knowledge.

[Understanding]

As for understanding, know that there is no way of access to God, سُبْحَانَهُ وَتَعَالَىٰ, except by transcending one's appetites and desires, abstaining from sensual delights, confining oneself to the bare necessities, and devoting oneself wholly to God, سُبْحَانَهُ, with every movement and rest. It was for this reason that the ascetics of previous religions used to isolate themselves from people and retire to mountains, preferring the solitude of the wilderness to the company of men, and thereby seeking intimacy with God تَعَالَىٰ. For the sake of God عَزَّوَجَلَّ they gave up worldly comforts and applied themselves to difficult spiritual practices in hopes of the hereafter. These are the ones whom God عَزَّوَجَلَّ praises in His book, saying

ذَٰلِكَ بِأَنَّ مِنْهُمْ قِسِّيسِينَ وَرُهْبَانًا وَأَنَّهُمْ لَا يَسْتَكْبِرُونَ ﴿٨٢﴾

That is because among them there are priests and monks, and because they are not arrogant [5:82].

When all of them were gone, and people started following their desires, and stopped devoting themselves to God عَزَّوَجَلَّ, and became lax concerning it, then God سُبْحَانَهُ وَتَعَالَىٰ, sent His Prophet Muḥammad صَلَّى ٱللَّٰهُ عَلَيْهِ وَسَلَّمَ to revive the way of the hereafter and to renew the *sunna* of the messengers عَلَيْهِمُ ٱلسَّلَامُ in traveling it. People of the earlier religions asked God's Messenger صَلَّى ٱللَّٰهُ عَلَيْهِ وَسَلَّمَ if the ways of monasticism and perpetual wandering were part of his *dīn* and he replied, "God has replaced them for us with combat for His cause and the repetition of the *takbīr* at every rise,"[35] by which he meant the pilgrimage.

35 Ibn al-Mubārak, *al-Jihād*, 17; al-Bukhārī, *Ṣaḥīḥ*, 1797; Muslim, *Ṣaḥīḥ*, 1344, with similar wording.

And when asked about those who perpetually wander in God's way, the Prophet ﷺ said, "They are the ones who fast."[36]

So God عَزَّوَجَلَّ has blessed this community by making the pilgrimage their monasticism, and has honored the ancient house by relating it to Himself, making it a destination for His servants, and making its surroundings a sanctuary for His house and a place of veneration. He has made ʿArafa a vast place of assembly leading to the courtyard of His sanctuary and has affirmed the sanctity of the place by forbidding hunting its [animals] and harming its trees. He has placed all this in the form of a great palace that visitors come to from every narrow ravine and steep pathway, [they come] disheveled, dusty, and humbled to the Lord of the house, submitted to His majesty, and subdued before His might, while at the same time acknowledging that He transcends confinement by a house or containment in any land, so that this [pilgrimage] might be an even greater expression of their acceptance and servanthood and a more perfect manifestation of their submission and obedience. Thus, certain rites are enjoined on them, [rites] like throwing stones at the pillars and running back and forth between Ṣafā and Marwā; the soul has no rapport with them, and the mind cannot decipher their meaning.

It is through such actions that the pilgrim demonstrates perfect submission and servitude. *Zakāt* is an expression of kindness and thus has a comprehensible aspect. Fasting breaks the appetites and desires, which are the instruments God's enemy [Satan], and allows more time for worship by eliminating other preoccupations. The bowing and prostration of the prayer express humility to God عَزَّوَجَلَّ through actions which are, in their very form, humbling and afford the soul intimacy in the veneration of God عَزَّوَجَلَّ.

But in running to and fro in the course [between Ṣafā and Marwā], throwing stones at the pillars, or other similar actions, there is no portion in which souls might take pleasure, no moment of intimacy for the affective nature, and no intelligible meaning for the mind. And so, the only motivation to perform these actions is the command itself and the intention to comply with the obligatory command . . . simply follow it. The discursive mind is set aside, and

36 Al-Ḥākim al-Nīsābūrī, *al-Mustadrak*, 2:335; al-Bayhaqī, *al-Sunan al-kubrā*, 4:305.

the soul and affective nature are turned away from their places of comfort. For if all this were readily comprehensible to the mind, the affective nature would incline toward it and that inclination would then become the support and motive for carrying out the commandment, and it would almost cease being an expression of submission and servanthood to God. But the Messenger ﷺ of God said, especially with regard to the pilgrimage, "Here I am at Your service on a pilgrimage in truth, in complete devotion and submission,"[37] and he did not say this for the prayer or any other [act of devotion].

If the wisdom of God تَعَالَىٰ has decreed that the salvation of human beings is linked to actions that are contrary to their natural inclinations and according to law (*sharīʿa*) they [must] perform these actions repeatedly in submission and fulfillment of the requirements of devotion . . . then those [actions] which are inaccessible [to human understanding] are the most effective kind of worship for purifying the soul and turning it away from fulfilling its inclinations and toward fulfilling the requirements of servanthood. If you grasp this, then you will understand that people's amazement concerning these wondrous actions arises from the fact that the mysteries of worship escaped them.

This much should suffice to give some understanding of the principle of the pilgrimage, God تَعَالَىٰ willing.

[Longing]

As for the longing [to complete it], this arises after understanding and realizing that the house is truly the house of God عَزَّوَجَلَّ, and that it is like a royal residence, and that one who intends to travel there intends to travel to God and one who visits it is visiting God عَزَّوَجَلَّ. Whoever intends to travel to the house in this world deserves for his visit not to be in vain and to be granted its object, the vision of God's noble countenance in the abode of eternity when it is his appointed time. For the limited and corporal eye we possess in this earthly abode is not made to receive the light of looking on the countenance of God عَزَّوَجَلَّ. It does not have the strength to bear it,

37 Al-Ramhurmuzī, *al-Muḥaddith al-fāṣil*, 624; and al-Khaṭīb al-Baghdādī, *Tārīkh Baghdād*, 14:218.

nor is it prepared—due to it finite nature—to be adorned by such a vision. It is in the abode of the hereafter, when it has been granted immortality and transcended the causes of change and corruption, that it will be ready to behold that sight, but by traveling to the sacred house and looking on it, it comes to merit the right to meet the Lord of the house, by the grace of [His] noble promise.

To be sure, the longing to meet God عَزَّوَجَلَّ will give rise to a longing for all the means that lead to that meeting, for the lover longs for everything that is connected with his beloved, and since the house is connected to God عَزَّوَجَلَّ, that in itself is enough to make one yearn for it, quite apart from seeking any promised reward [in the hereafter].

[Resolve]

As for the resolve [to set out], the pilgrim should know that in making this resolution, he is proposing to separate from his family and homeland and forsaking his desires and pleasures as he turns to visit the house of God عَزَّوَجَلَّ.

He should esteem both the house itself and the Lord of the house and he should know that he has resolved to undertake something that is of great importance and [entails] great peril. Whoever seeks to accomplish such a thing is putting himself in danger, so he should be sure that his intention is purely for the sake of God تَعَالَى, and [his intention] is untainted by ostentation or a desire to be known.

And he should fully realize that nothing will be accepted of his intention or his actions except what is done in sincerity and truth, and that there is no worse offense than to set out for the house of the sovereign and His sanctuary for any other purpose than to visit Him. So, he should verify his resolve in himself, and verify his sincerity, and that sincerity lies in avoiding anything that hints of a desire to be seen or a desire for fame. He should be careful to replace what is lower with something that is higher.

[Attachments]

As for severing attachments, this means [first], making restitution to anyone he has wronged while at the same time sincerely repenting to God تَعَالَى for all [his] sins. Every wrong he has done to another is an attachment, and every attachment is like having a creditor with you, hanging onto your neck, and crying out, "Where are you headed? Are you headed for the house of the King of kings, when you have scornfully neglected His commandment in this, your home? Are you not ashamed to approach Him like a rebellious servant, lest He reject you and not receive you?"

If you truly want your visit to be accepted, then follow His commandments, rectify any injustices you have committed, turn to Him in repentance first for all your sins, and then sever your heart's connection to what is behind you. In doing this, you will be one who turns his whole heart in God's direction, even as you turn your face in the direction of His house. But if you fail to do this, you will gain nothing from your journey except weariness and hardship at its start and dismissal and rejection at its end.

The pilgrim should sever all ties with his homeland, cut himself off completely, and not expect to return. He should write his will for his family and children, for a traveler and his wealth are in danger unless God تَعَالَىٰ protects them.

And while severing these attachments in order to make the journey of the pilgrimage, he should remember the attachments that will be severed when he journeys to the hereafter, for he will soon face [that]. All that he accomplishes for this journey should be in the hope of making that journey easier, for that is the journey to the final abode—and to *Him is the [final] destination* [Q. 5:18, 42:15, 64:3]. As he makes preparations for this journey of pilgrimage, he should not forget that [much longer] journey.

[Provisions]

As for provisions, he should purchase these from a lawful source. If the pilgrim feels that he needs to take along a lot, and wants to take something that will last for the entire journey, something that will not perish before he reaches his destination, then he should remember that the journey to the hereafter is much longer and that the only provision he may take for it is piety (*taqwā*). Whatever else he thinks will be his provision will be left behind at death and [will] not go with him. It will be like trying to travel with fresh food that goes bad during the first stage of the journey, so that when the time of need arises, the traveler is helpless and in need.

He should beware, therefore, that the deeds which he counts on for his provision in the hereafter are not those that vanish at death, spoiled by the stain of hypocrisy and the turbidity of neglect.

[Conveyances]

As for the mount [to be ridden on the journey], when the pilgrim finds a good one he should give thanks to God تَعَالَىٰ from the bottom of his heart for having put under his control an animal that will relieve him of some of his burdens and lessen for him the hardships of the journey. And at that same time, he should recall the mount that will bear him to the abode of the hereafter, and by this, I mean the funeral bier on which he will be carried to his grave. In one respect, the pilgrimage parallels the journey to the hereafter.

He should consider whether the journey he is about to make riding on this mount will serve him as provision for that other journey riding on that other mount—and how near to him that journey is! For all he knows, death may be so near that he will be riding on the funeral bier before he has time to ride on that camel. [The fact] that he will ride on that bier is certain, whereas securing the necessary means for the journey [to Mecca] is doubtful, so how can he be so careful concerning this journey [which may never happen], obtaining the provisions and choosing the right mount, while neglecting [to make preparations] for the journey which is sure to happen?

[Purchasing the *Iḥrām*]

As for purchasing the two cloths for *iḥrām*, when buying these, the pilgrim should bring to mind the shroud and being wrapped in it for burial. For when he nears the house of God تَعَالَىٰ, he will put on two cloths and yet he may not complete his journey to it, but [it] is certain that he will meet God تَعَالَىٰ wrapped in the cloth of his shroud.

Just as he does not go to meet the house of God عَزَّوَجَلَّ except after changing his ordinary dress and appearance, so too, after death, he will not meet God عَزَّوَجَلَّ except in a garment that is unlike any worn in this world, and that is the shroud. And the pilgrim's garb is like that: unsewn cloth, without legs or sleeves, exactly like a shroud.

[Departure]

As for leaving his homeland, in doing this he should know that he is separating himself from family and home, heading toward God عَزَّوَجَلَّ, on a journey unlike any other journey in this world. So in his heart he should prepare for what he intends, where he is heading, and whom he intends to visit. He should know that he is heading to the King of kings, among a host of [the King's] visitors who were called and then answered, who were made to long for this journey and then longed for it, who were awakened and then awoke, who have severed their attachments, separated themselves from people, and set out for the house of God عَزَّوَجَلَّ, splendid in its majesty and lofty in esteem, consoling themselves by encountering the house, in place of the Lord of the house, that they might be granted their ultimate wish and be blessed by the vision of their guardian Lord.

The pilgrim should keep the hope of arrival and the hope of acceptance present in his heart, not by virtue of his deeds in journeying far from his family and possessions, but rather by trusting in God's grace and being hopeful that He will keep His promise to those who visit His house and if death should overtake him [the pilgrim] on the way, he will meet God عَزَّوَجَلَّ waiting for his arrival, even as He has said عَزَّوَجَلَّ,

وَمَن يَخْرُجْ مِنۢ بَيْتِهِۦ مُهَاجِرًا إِلَى ٱللَّهِ وَرَسُولِهِۦ ثُمَّ يُدْرِكْهُ ٱلْمَوْتُ فَقَدْ وَقَعَ أَجْرُهُۥ عَلَى ٱللَّهِ

... And whoever leaves his home as an emigrant to God and His Messenger and then death overtakes him—his reward has already become incumbent upon God [4:100].

[The Journey]

As for entering the wilderness on the way to the stations and beholding the many steep mountain paths, the pilgrim should bring to mind the crossing at death between this world and the place of gathering on the day of resurrection, and the many dreadful things and trials that are in between.

Let his dread of highway robbers remind him of the dread of being questioned by Munkar and Nakīr,[38] and let the wild beasts of the wilderness remind him of the scorpions and worms of the grave, and its vipers and serpents. Let his isolation from family and friends remind him of the desolation of the grave itself, and its distress and its solitude.

[In short], all that he fears on this journey should be expressed in his words and actions, [and they will] become his provision [against] the torments of the grave.

[Entering *Iḥrām*]

As for entering *iḥrām* and beginning the pilgrim's call (*talbiyya*) from the station onward, the pilgrim should know that in doing so, he is answering the call of God عَزَّوَجَلَّ. He should hope to be accepted and fear being told, "Neither service nor happiness are yours."[39] He should vacillate between hope and fear, relinquish [his claim] to any power and strength, and rely wholly on the grace of God عَزَّوَجَلَّ and His infinite generosity. When the *talbiyya* begins, that is the real starting point and place of danger.

Sufyān b. ʿUyayna said,

> ʿAlī b. al-Ḥusayn رَضِيَ ٱللَّهُ عَنْهُمَا went on pilgrimage. When he entered *iḥrām* and settled on his camel, he suddenly grew pale and began to tremble and shake so much that he was unable to utter the *talbiyya*. When he was asked why did you not [say] the *talbiyya*, he answered, "Because I so dread it being said to me 'Neither service nor happiness be yours.'" When he finally managed to say it, he passed out and fell from his camel, and this continued to happen to him until he had completed his pilgrimage.

And Aḥmad b. Abī l-Ḥawārī said,

38 The two angels that question the soul in the grave.

39 *Lā labayka wa-lā saʿdayka*! This is the negation of the pilgrims' call *Labayka wa-saʿdayka!* (lit., "Here I am [O Lord] at Your service and for Your pleasure").

> I was with Abū Sulaymān al-Dārānī رَضِيَ ٱللَّهُ عَنْهُ when he wished to enter *iḥrām*, but he did not begin to utter the *talbiyya* until we had traveled a mile and when he did, he lost all consciousness for a time. When he came to, I said "O Aḥmad! God, سُبْحَانَهُ, said by inspiration to Moses عَلَيْهِ ٱلسَّلَامُ, 'Command the oppressor among the children of Israel not to mention much My name, for if [in their wrongdoing] they mention Me, I mention them with a curse.' Alas, dear Aḥmad, it has reached me that God عَزَّ وَجَلَّ says to those who make the pilgrimage with illicit gains, "Neither service nor happiness is yours until you return what you borrowed." And we cannot be sure that this will not be said to us![40]

The pilgrim should also remember when he raises his voice with the others in the *talbiyya* at the stations, that they are answering the call of God تَعَالَىٰ when He said [to Abraham],

وَأَذِّن فِي ٱلنَّاسِ بِٱلْحَجِّ

And proclaim to the people the ḥajj [22:27]

as well as the trumpet blast that will summon all creatures, as they are resurrected from the graves and brought to the crowded plain of the resurrection, answering [again] the call of God تَعَالَىٰ, to be divided into those who are graced by nearness and those who have earned God's wrath, those who are accepted and those who are rejected, initially going to and fro between hope and fear just like the pilgrims at the station who do not know whether or not they will be given the chance to complete the pilgrimage and have it accepted.

[**Mecca**]

As for entering Mecca, at this time the pilgrim should remember that he has arrived at a secure sanctuary so in doing so he should hope that he will be safe from the chastisement of God تَعَالَىٰ. He should fear that he may not merit nearness [to God], such that his entry into the sanctuary is in vain and merits chastisement. But at all

40 Al-Dīnawarī, *al-Majālis wa-jawāhir al-ʿilm*, 136; Ibn ʿAsākir, *Tārīkh madinat Dimashq*, 41:278.

times, his hope should be foremost in his soul, for God's generosity is profound, the Lord is All-Compassionate, the nobility of the house is tremendous, the right of the visitor is respected, and the safety promised to those who seek its protection is not lost.

[Seeing the House]

As for setting eyes on the house, at this moment your heart should be so filled with consciousness of the greatness of the Kaʿba that it would be as if you were seeing the Lord of the house. And hope, at the same time, that God will bless you with the vision of His noble countenance, just as He has blessed you with the vision of His exalted house. Give thanks to Him for bringing you to this place, and for permitting you to be among the assembly of those who visit Him.

And at the same time remember the people on the day of resurrection surging forth toward heaven, all hoping to enter, and [remember] that some will be permitted and others turned away, just as the pilgrims are divided into those whose pilgrimage is accepted and those whose [pilgrimage] is rejected. Do not forget—in everything you see—to recall the matters of the hereafter, for all the conditions experienced in the pilgrimage are reflections of the conditions of the hereafter.

[The *Ṭawāf*]

As for the *ṭawāf*, know that this is a prayer and so, as you are making it, your heart should be filled with humble reverence, fear, hope, and love as we have mentioned in the *Mysteries of Prayer*. Know too that in making circumambulations around the house you are like God's angels drawn near, who encompass the throne and circle around it.

And do not suppose that the purpose of this action is for your physical form to go around the house. Rather, the true purpose is the *ṭawāf* of your heart through the invocation of the Lord of the house, so do not start your invocation except from Him and do not end it except with Him, just as your *ṭawāf* starts from the house and ends at the house.

Know that the noblest *ṭawāf* is a heart that circles the Lord's presence. The house is but a visible symbol in this realm of dominion for that presence which eyes cannot behold, for it exists in the dominion of the heavens (*ʿālam al-malakūt*). In a similar manner, for the one to whom God opens the door, our physical body is just a visible symbol of the heart, which eyes cannot see, since it exists in the hidden realm (*ʿālam al-ghayb*), the realm of the dominions. This correspondence is reflected in the fact that it is said that the much-frequented house[41] is in the heavens above the Kaʿba and the heavenly *ṭawāf* of the angels around it is like the human *ṭawāf* around this house. Since the degree of most people falls far short of making such a *ṭawāf*, they are commanded to imitate it as much as they can and are promised that, "He who imitates a folk becomes one of them."[42] And the one who is able to make such a *ṭawāf* is one of those about whom it has been said, "The Kaʿba visits him and makes *ṭawāf* around him." This is according to what some of those with spiritual vision saw happen with some of the friends of God, سُبْحَانَهُ وَتَعَالَىٰ.

[The Black Stone]

As for touching the black stone, the moment you do this, be assured that you are making a pact of allegiance to God عَزَّوَجَلَّ and vowing to obey Him.[43] Resolve to fulfill your pact, for whoever breaks such a pact deserves God's anger. Ibn ʿAbbās رَضِيَ ٱللَّهُ عَنْهُمَا related that the Prophet صَلَّى ٱللَّهُ عَلَيْهِ وَسَلَّمَ said, "The black stone is the right hand of God عَزَّوَجَلَّ on earth. With it He shakes hands with His creatures, just as a man shakes hands with his brother."[44]

[The Curtain]

As for clinging to the curtains of the Kaʿba, and cleaving to Multazim, in doing the latter your intention should be to draw near to the house and to the Lord of the house in love and yearning, and

41 *Al-bayt al-maʿmūr* is mentioned in Q. 52:4. According to *ḥadīth*s in al-Bukhārī, Muslim, and many other collections, during the ascension (*miʿrāj*), the angel Gabriel showed the Prophet صَلَّى ٱللَّهُ عَلَيْهِ وَسَلَّمَ, "Every day seventy thousand angels enter it and then they leave and never return." Al-Bukhārī, *Ṣaḥīḥ*, 2038; Muslim, *Ṣaḥīḥ*, 164. Other traditions state that *al-bayt al-maʿmūr* is in the heavens above the Kaʿba.

42 Abū Dāwūd, *Sunan*, 4031.

43 Traditionally, a pact is symbolized by taking the hand of the one to whom you are swearing allegiance.

44 Al-Azraqī, *Akhbār Makka*, 1:257; al-Ḥākim al-Nīsābūrī, *al-Mustadrak*, 1:457.

to seek blessing through this physical touch, hoping thereby that every part of your body that comes in contact with the house may be protected from the fire.

And as you cling to the curtains, your intention should be to persist in asking God's forgiveness and to beg for safety, just as someone who has sinned against another human being clings to the clothes [of the wronged person] while imploring his pardon to show him that he [the sinner] has no refuge except from him [the wronged person] and no shelter except for his pardon and generosity, and that he [the sinner] will not let go of the hem of his [the wronged person] garment until he [the sinner] is forgiven and promised safety in the future.

[The Course]

As for running between Ṣafā and Marwā in the entrance of the house, this is like the going and coming, again and again, of a servant in the antechamber of the king. In doing this, the pilgrim demonstrates his devotion to service and his hope that [God] will look on him with an eye to mercy, just as one who comes into the presence of a king leaves without knowing whether, in respect to his case, the king has decided to accept or reject [him]. And so he keeps going back to the open courtyard time and time again, hoping that he may be forgiven the second time if he was not [forgiven] the first [time].

And as he goes back and forth [in laps] between Ṣafā and Marwā he should also call to mind how he himself may go back and forth between the two pans of the scale on the open plain of the resurrection. He should let Ṣafā represent the pan holding his good deeds and Marwā the pan holding his bad ones. He should bring to mind his uncertainty about the two as he looks to see which is heavier, which is lighter, suspended between punishment and forgiveness.

[ʿArafa]

As for standing at ʿArafa, when you see the throngs of people, and hear the voices raised in so many languages, and see them following their various leaders through the rites, imitating their actions and following their ways, then bring to mind the plain of the resurrection and the gathering of the communities with their prophets and leaders, each community following its prophet, aspiring for his intercession, and wavering with equal uncertainty between rejection and acceptance.

And after you have brought all this to mind, your heart should cleave to supplication and humility to God عَزَّوَجَلَّ [hoping] that you may be resurrected in the company of those who win the race. Be certain that your hope will be fulfilled, for that is a noble place to stand and mercy from the presence of the majestic reaches all creatures by way of the hearts of the mainstays (*awtād*) of the earth. That place of standing is never devoid of the substitutes (*abdāl*)[45] or the saintly, the people of the heart. When their aspirations are gathered together, and their hearts are focused solely on humility before God and [making] supplications, and their hands are raised up toward God تَعَالَى, and their necks are stretched toward Him, and their eyes are lifted heavenward, and the sole aspiration of all [of them] is to seek [God's] mercy, then do not suppose in the least that God would disappoint them, or let their efforts be in vain, or withhold His mercy from them. This is why it has been said, "The most grievous sin is for someone to be present at ʿArafa and think that God تَعَالَى will not forgive him."[46]

It is as if the gathering of [those with] these aspirations, strengthened by the presence of the *abdāl* and *awtād* from around the world were indeed the mystery of the pilgrimage and its ultimate purpose. There is no better method by which to attract the mercy of God سُبْحَانَهُ, than through the gathering of [people with] aspirations and the mutual support of hearts, at one time, and on one plain.

[The Pebbles]

As for casting pebbles at the pillars, in doing this your intention should be obedience to God's commandment, to show your submission and servanthood, and your fervor in the simple act of obedience, without any [perceivable] benefit for the mind or the ego.

Rather, make it your pure intention to imitate Abraham عَلَيْهِ ٱلسَّلَامُ, since it was in this place that Iblīs, may God curse him, appeared

---

45 See 12 n.44.

46 A similar saying is narrated as a *ḥadīth*: "The most sinful of people is someone who stands at ʿArafa and thinks that God تَعَالَى will not forgive him"; see 6.

to him who tried to cast doubt on his [Abraham's] pilgrimage and tempt him toward sin. So God تَعَالَىٰ commanded him [Abraham] to cast stones [at Iblīs] to repel him and thwart his hopes.

And if you should think, at that moment, "Satan actually appeared to him [Abraham]. He actually saw him, and that is why he threw stones at him, but Satan is not showing himself to me," then know that this very notion is from Satan, who cast it into your heart to undermine your resolve to cast the pebbles and to make it appear to you as a useless act, a kind of game, so why should you be bothered with it?

So drive him [Satan] from your soul, cast the stones with fervor, and throw his designs back in his face. And know that while outwardly you are casting pebbles at ʿAqaba pillar, in reality you are throwing them in the face of Satan and dealing him a mortal blow, for the only way to demean him is by obeying the commands of God سُبْحَانَهُ, in pure veneration, free of ego or rationalization.

[The Sacrifice]

And as for the sacrifice, know that this is a means of drawing close to God تَعَالَىٰ by virtue of compliance, so do the slaughtering perfectly, divide its meat into parts, and hope that for each part [you give to the poor] God will deliver a part of you from the fire, for such is a promise passed down, so that the larger the sacrificial animal and fuller its parts, the more complete will be your ransom from the fire.[47]

[Medina]

As for the visit to Medina, when your eyes catch a glimpse of its walls, recall that this is the town which God عَزَّوَجَلَّ chose for His Prophet صَلَّىٱللَّهُعَلَيْهِوَسَلَّمَ and made his place of migration, and that this was his home when he promulgated the duties which his Lord عَزَّوَجَلَّ enjoined as well as his *sunna*, where he strove against his enemies and proclaimed his *dīn* until God عَزَّوَجَلَّ caused him to pass away from this world.

---

47 Al-Ghazālī may be referring to a *ḥadīth* attributed to Fāṭima رَضِيَٱللَّهُعَنْهَا concerning the sacrifice.

Then God made it his burial ground and the burial ground of his two Companions[48] who upheld the truth after him. Then imagine to yourself the places where the Messenger صَلَّى ٱللَّٰهُ عَلَيْهِ وَسَلَّمَ of God placed his feet as his went about the city and know that wherever your feet may tread, his precious feet walked there too. So take each step with dignity and awe.

Recall his [Prophet Muḥammad] walking and his steps on its roads and try to picture the humble reverence of his gait while he carried in his heart the immense knowledge which God سُبْحَانَهُ, placed there, and how God تَعَالَىٰ exalted his [the Messenger's] remembrance along with His remembrance so that they are connected.[49] Call to mind as well how God rendered futile the deeds of those who showed him disrespect, even if it was only by raising their voices louder than his.[50]

Then remember the grace which God bestowed on those who were able to be his Companions and fortunate enough to see him and to hear his words. At the same time, feel regret that you did not have the chance to be in his presence and the presence of his Companions رَضِيَ ٱللَّٰهُ عَنْهُمْ.

Call to mind that you have missed seeing him in this world, but seeing him in the hereafter may be a peril for you. For it may be that you will see him [the Prophet and you will be] full of regret for having lost his [the Prophet's] acceptance through your bad deeds, even as he صَلَّى ٱللَّٰهُ عَلَيْهِ وَسَلَّمَ said,

> God will raise up a certain people to me who will say, "O Muḥammad! O Muḥammad!" And I will say, "O Lord, these are my companions!" But He will answer, "You do not know what they innovated after you." Then he will say, "Let them be far removed from me!"[51]

---

48 This refers to Abū Bakr and ʿUmar.

49 That is, in the twofold testimony, "There is no god but God and Muḥammad is the Messenger of God," there is mention of the name of God and the name of the Prophet صَلَّى ٱللَّٰهُ عَلَيْهِ وَسَلَّمَ.

50 The Qurʾān states, *O you who have believed, do not raise your voices above the voice of the Prophet or be loud to him in speech like the loudness of some of you to others, lest your deeds become worthless while you perceive not* [49:2].

51 Al-Bukhārī, *Ṣaḥīḥ*, 6585; Muslim, *Ṣaḥīḥ*, 249.

If you have ceased to respect the sanctity of his law, even if it is about something small, do not consider yourself safe from something coming between you and him [the Prophet], or from losing his intercession.

Yet at the same time, your hope should be great that God will not keep you from him [the Prophet] after having granted you faith and taken you away from your homeland for the purpose of visiting him. For [you have done this] not for commerce or for worldly gain, but purely for the love you have for him and your longing to look on his traces and on the wall of his tomb. For since you were deprived of the chance to see him in this world, you embarked on this journey for that reason alone, and if this was your purpose, then you surely deserve for God to look on you with mercy.

When you reach the mosque, you should recall that this was the place chosen by God عَزَّوَجَلَّ for His Prophet صَلَّىٱللَّهُعَلَيْهِوَسَلَّمَ and for those first and most excellent of Muslims. Remember too that the laws enjoined by God سُبْحَانَهُ, were first established on this ground, and that the best of God's creatures, living or dead, are gathered here.

Therefore, your hope should be great that God سُبْحَانَهُ, will have mercy on you as you enter it, and then enter it with humble reverence and veneration. How worthy a place to put humility in the heart of every believer! As Abū Sulaymān is reported to have said,

> Uways al-Qarnī رَحِمَهُٱللَّهُ made the pilgrimage and then entered Medina. As he stood at the door of the mosque, someone said to him, "This is the tomb of the Prophet صَلَّىٱللَّهُعَلَيْهِوَسَلَّمَ," and he fell unconscious. When he came to he said, "Take me outside, for it is impossible for me to feel any pleasure in a town where Muḥammad صَلَّىٱللَّهُعَلَيْهِوَسَلَّمَ lies buried!"[52]

As for visiting God's Messenger صَلَّىٱللَّهُعَلَيْهِوَسَلَّمَ, you should stand before him in the manner we have described, visiting him in death as you would have visited him in life.

Do not approach his tomb except as you would have approached his noble person in life and just as you would see it as a sign of respect not to touch or kiss his person [in life, so behave with the same respect].

---

52 Abū Nuʿaym, *Ḥilya*, 9:262; Ibn ʿAsākir, *Tārīkh madinat Dimashq*, 9:450.

Rather, you would have stood at a respectful distance before him, and this is what you should do now. Indeed, touching and kissing shrines is a custom of the Christians and Jews.

And know that he is aware of your presence, of your standing there and of your visit, and [he knows] that your greetings and prayers of blessings are conveyed to him.

Picture in your mind his noble form lying in the tomb before you and sense his exalted rank in your heart.

For he صَلَّى ٱللَّهُ عَلَيْهِ وَسَلَّمَ is reported to have said that God تَعَالَىٰ has appointed for his tomb an angel who conveys to him the salutations of anyone of his community who greets him[53] and this refers to the case of those not actually present there, so what about someone who has left his homeland and crossed the wilderness out of longing to meet him, who is content merely to look on his noble shrine since he had not been given the chance to see his noble face in life?

And he said صَلَّى ٱللَّهُ عَلَيْهِ وَسَلَّمَ "He who blesses me once God blesses tenfold."[54] This refers to the reward for verbally invoking blessings on him صَلَّى ٱللَّهُ عَلَيْهِ وَسَلَّمَ, so what about someone who comes to visit him in person?

After this, you should go to the *minbar* of God's Messenger صَلَّى ٱللَّهُ عَلَيْهِ وَسَلَّمَ and picture him ascending it.

Imagine, too, his radiant beauty as he stood there, surrounded by the Emigrants (Muhājirīn) and Helpers (Anṣār) رَضِيَ ٱللَّهُ عَنْهُمْ, and encouraged them toward obedience to God عَزَّ وَجَلَّ.

And finally, ask God عَزَّ وَجَلَّ that you not be separated from him on the day of resurrection.

Such are the duties of the heart at all stages of the pilgrimage.

When all these have been completed, he [the pilgrim] should keep concern, sadness, and fear in his heart, for he does not know whether his pilgrimage has been accepted and he has been confirmed as part of the company of the beloved, or [if it has been] rejected and he has been left among the banished.

He will come to know this, however, from his heart and deeds.

If he finds his heart turning away from this abode of delusions and inclining toward the abode of intimacy with God, سُبْحَانَهُ وَتَعَالَىٰ

53 Al-Bayhaqī, *Shuʿab al-īmān*, 2773; Ibn ʿAsākir, *Tārīkh madinat Dimashq*, 54:301.

54 Muslim, *Ṣaḥīḥ*, 408.

and finds that his conduct fills the balance[55] of the law, then he may have confidence that he has found acceptance, for God تَعَالَىٰ accepts only those He loves.

The one He loves, He takes care of and manifests the signs of His love, protecting him from the power of His enemy Iblīs, may God curse him.

If these signs are apparent, they point to acceptance and if not, then it is likely that the only recompense the pilgrim has earned from his journey is simply fatigue and toil, and we seek refuge from that in God, سُبْحَانَهُ وَتَعَالَىٰ.

Here ends *The Book on the Mysteries of the Pilgrimage and Its Important Elements*, book 7 of the Quarter of Worship from the *Revival of the Religious Sciences*. Praise be to God, Lord of the worlds, praise in abundance, pure and blessed, as is His due. He is our sufficiency and the best in whom to put our trust.

And may blessings and salutations be on the best of creation, our master Muḥammad, the unlettered prophet, and on his pure family, as often as those who remember mention him and as often those who are negligent forget to mention him! Following this is the *Book on the Manners of Reciting the Qurʾān*, [book 8 of the Quarter of Worship from the *Revival of the Religious Sciences*].

55 This alludes to filling the scales of the balance on the day of judgment; it is a reminder to increase one's good deeds after returning home from the pilgrimage.

Bibliography

Works in Western Languages

al-Ghazālī, Abū Ḥāmid Muḥammad. *The Mysteries of Purification: Kitāb asrār al-ṭahāra. Book 3 of The Revival of the Religious Sciences.* Translated by M. Fouad Aresmouk and M. Abdurrahman Fitzgerald. Louisville, KY: Fons Vitae, 2017.

al-Ghazālī, Abū Ḥāmid Muḥammad. *The Mysteries of Prayer: Kitāb asrār al-ṣalāt. Book 4 of The Revival of the Religious Sciences.* Translated by M. Abdurrahman Fitzgerald. Louisville, KY: Fons Vitae, 2018.

Lings, Martin. *Muhammad: His Life Based on the Earliest Sources.* Cambridge: Islamic Texts Society, 1983.

al-Mubarakpuri, Safi-ur-Rahman. *ar-Raheeq al-makhtūm (The sealed nectar).* Riyadh: Maktaba Dar-us-Salam, 1996.

al-Tustarī, Sahl b. ʿAbdallāh. Tafsīr al-Tustarī. Translated by Annabel Keeler and Ali Keeler. Louisville, KY: Royal Aal al-Bayt Institute for Islamic Thought and Fons Vitae, 2011.

Works in Arabic

ʿAbd al-Razzāq b. Hammām al-Ṣanʿānī. *al-Muṣannaf.* Edited by Ḥabīb al-Raḥmān al-ʿAẓamī. Beirut: Maktab al-Islāmī, 1983.

Abū Dāwūd, Sulaymān b. al-Ashaʿth al-Sijistānī. *al-Murāsil.* Edited by ʿAbdallāh Musāʿid al-Zaharānī. Riyadh: Dār al-Ṣumayʿī, 2001.

Abū Dāwūd, Sulaymān b. al-Ashaʿth al-Sijistānī. *Sunan Abū Dāwūd.* Edited by ʿIzzat ʿAbīd al-Daʿās and ʿĀdil al-Sayyid. Beirut: Dār Ibn Ḥazm, 1997.

Abū Nuʿaym al-Iṣbahānī, Aḥmad b. ʿAbdallāh. *Ḥilyat al-awliyāʾ wa-ṭabaqāt al-aṣfiyāʾ.* Cairo: Maṭbaʿāt al-Saʿāda wa-l-Khānijī, 1357/1938; repr. Beirut: Dār al-Kitāb al-ʿArabī, 1987.

Abū Nuʿaym al-Iṣbahānī, Aḥmad b. ʿAbdallāh. *Tārīkh Iṣbahān.* Edited by Sayyid Kusrawī Ḥasan. Beirut: Dār al-Kutub al-ʿIlmiyya, 1990.

Abū Shaykh, ʿAbdallāh b. Muḥammad. *Ṭabaqāt al-muḥaddithīn.* Edited by ʿAbd al-Ghafūr al-Balūshī. Beirut: Muʾassassat al-Risāla, 1992.

Abū Ṭālib al-Makkī, Muḥammad b. ʿAlī. *Qūt al-qulūb*. Edited by Muḥammad al-Zaharī al-Ghumurāwī. Cairo: al-Maṭbaʿat al-Mayymaniyya, 1310/1893. Repr. Beirut: Dār Ṣādir/Dār al-Fikr, n.d.

al-Ālūsī, Abū l-Thanāʾ Maḥmūd b. ʿAbdallāh al-Ḥusaynī. *Tafsīr al-Ālūsī: Rūḥ al-maʿānī fī tafsīr al-qurʾān al-ʿaẓīm wa-l-sabʿ al-mathānī*. Beirut: Dār Iḥyāʾ al-Turath al-ʿArabī, 1985.

al-Azraqī, Muḥammad b. ʿAbdallāh b. Aḥmad. *Akhbār Makka wa-mā jaʾa fīhā min al-āthār*. Edited by ʿAlī ʿUmar. Cairo: Makatabat al-Thaqāfa al-Dīniyya, 2004.

al-Baghawī, Ḥusayn b. Masʿūd. *Maʿālim al-tanzīl fī tafsīr al-Qurʾān*. Edited by Muḥammad ʿAbdallāh al-Nimr et. al. Riyadh: Dār Ṭayyba, 1409–12/1988–91.

al-Bayhaqī, Aḥmad b. al-Ḥusayn. *Shuʿab al-īmān*. Edited by Muḥammad al-Saʿīd b. Basyūnī Zaghlūl. Beirut: Dār al-Kutub al-ʿIlmiyyya, 2000.

al-Bayhaqī, Aḥmad b. al-Ḥusayn. *al-Sunan al-kubrā*. Beirut: Dār al-Maʿrifa, 1356.

al-Bukhārī, Muḥammad b. Ismāʿīl. *Ṣaḥīḥ al-Bukhārī*. Būlāq, 1311–13 [repr. Beirut: Dār Ṭawq al-Najāt, 1422/2001].

al-Dāraquṭnī, ʿAlī b. ʿUmar. *Sunan al-Dāraquṭnī*. Edited by ʿAbdallāh Hashim Yamānī. Beirut: Dār al-Maʿrifa, 1966 [repr.].

al-Dārimī, ʿAbdallāh b. ʿAbd al-Raḥmān. *Musnad al-Dārimī = Sunan*. Edited by Ḥusayn Salīm Asad al-Dārānī. Riyadh: Dār al-Mughnī, 2000.

al-Daylamī, Shīrawayh b. Shahdār. *al-Firdaws bi-maʾthūr al-khiṭṭāb = Musnad al-firdaws*. Edited by Saʿīd b. Basyūnī Zaghlūl. Beirut: Dār al-Kutub al-ʿIlmiyya, 1986.

al-Dīnawarī, Aḥmad b. Marwān b. Muḥammad, *al-Majālisa wa-jawāhir al-ʿilm*. Beirut: Dār Ibn Ḥazm, 2002.

al-Fāhikī, Muḥammad b. Isḥāq al-ʿAbbās. *Akhbār Makka fī qadim al-dahr wa-ḥadīth*. Edited by ʿAbd al-Malik ʿAbdallāh Dahayyash. Beirut: Dār Khiḍr, 1414.

al-Ḥākim al-Nīsābūrī, Muḥammad b. ʿAbdallāh. *al-Mustadrak ʿalā l-Ṣaḥiḥayn*. Hyderabad: Dāʾirat al-Maʿārif al-Niẓāmiyya, 1335/1917 [repr. Beirut: Dār al-Maʿrifa, n.d.].

al-Ḥakīm al-Tirmidhī, Muḥammad b. ʿAlī. *Nawādir al-uṣūl*. Beirut: Dār Ṣādir, n.d. [repr. Cairo, 1293/1876 edition].

al-Ḥarbī, Ibrāhīm b. Isḥāq. *Gharīb al-ḥadīth*. Edited by Sulaymān b. al-Āyyīd. Mecca: Jāmaʿat Umm al-Qūrra, 1985.

Ibn ʿAbd al-Barr, Yūsuf b. ʿAbdallāh al-Nimrī. *Bahjat al-majālis*. Edited by Muḥammad Mursī al-Khūrī. Beirut: Dār al-Kutub al-ʿIlmiyya, 1981.

Ibn Abī ʿArūba, Saʿīd. *Manāsik*. Edited by ʿĀmr Ṣabrī. Beirut: Dār al-Bashāʾir al-Islāmiyya, 2000.

Ibn Abī l-Dunyā, ʿAbdallāh b. Muḥammad al-Qurashī. *al-Ṣamt wa-ādāb al-lisān*. Edited by Najm ʿAbd al-Raḥmān Khalaf. Beirut: Dār al-Gharb al-Islāmī, 1986.

Ibn Abī Shayba, ʿAbdallāh b. Muḥammad. *al-Muṣannaf*. Edited by Muḥammad ʿAwāmma. Jedda: Dār al-Minhāj, 2006.

Ibn ʿAdī = ʿAbdallāh b. ʿAdī l-Jurjānī. *al-Kāmil fī ḍuʿafāʾ al-rijāl*. Edited by Suhayl Zakkār and Yaḥyā Mukhtār Ghazāwī. Beirut: Dār al-Fikr, 1988.

Ibn ʿAsākir, ʿAlī b. al-Ḥasan. *Tārīkh madīnat Dimashq*. Edited by Muḥibb al-Dīn ʿUmar b. Gharāma al-ʿUmrāwī. Beirut: Dār al-Fikr, 1995.

Ibn Ḥanbal = Aḥmad b. Ḥanbal. *Musnad al-Imām Aḥmad b. Ḥanbal*. Edited by Shuʿayb al-Arnāʾūṭ. Beirut: Muʾassasat al-Risāla, 1995.

Ibn Ḥibbān, Abū Hatim Muḥammad al-Tamīmī l-Bustī. *Ṣaḥīḥ*. Edited by Shuʿayb al-Arnāʾūṭ. Beirut: Muʿassasat al-Risāla, 1993.

Ibn al-Jawzī, ʿAbd al-Raḥmān b. ʿAlī. *Ṣifat al-ṣafwa*. Edited by ʿAbd al-Salām Hārūn. Beirut: Muʾassassa al-Kutub al-Thaqāfiyya, 1992.

Ibn Khuzayma, Abū Bakr b. Muḥammad b. Isḥāq al-Nīsābūrī, *Ṣaḥīḥ Ibn Khuzayma*. Edited by Muḥammad Muṣṭafā al-ʿAẓamī. Beirut: al-Maktab al-Islāmī, 2003.

Ibn Mājah, Muḥammad b. Yazīd. *Sunan Ibn Mājah*. Edited by Muḥammad Fuʾād ʿAbd al-Bāqī. Cairo: Dār Iḥyāʾ al-Kutub al-ʿArabiyya, 1954.

Ibn al-Mubārak, ʿAbdallāh. *al-Jihād*. Edited by Nazīh Ḥamād. Riyadh: Dār al-Maṭbūʿāt al-Ḥadītha, n.d.

Ibn al-Mubārak, ʿAbdallāh. *Zuhd wa-l-raqāʾiq*. Edited by Ḥabīb al-Raḥmān al-ʿAẓamī. Beirut: Dār al-Kutub al-ʿIlmiyya, n.d.

al-Khaṭīb al-Baghdādī, Aḥmad b. ʿAlī, *al-Muttafiq wa-l-muftariq*. Edited by Dr. Muḥammad Ṣādiq Āyudin al-Ḥāmadī. Damascus: Dār al-Qādirī, 1997.

al-Khaṭīb al-Baghdādī, Aḥmad b. ʿAlī. *Tārīkh Baghdād*. Edited by Muṣṭafā ʿAbd al-Qādir ʿAṭā. Beirut: Dār al-Kutub al-ʿIlmiyya, 1997.

al-Lālakāʾī, Hibat Allāh b. al-Ḥasan. *Sharḥ uṣūl iʿtiqād ahl alsunna*. Edited by Aḥmad Saʿd al-Ghāmidī. Riyadh: Dār Ṭayyiba, 2005.

al-Maḥāmilī, al-Ḥusayn b. Ismāʿīl. *al-Duʿāʾ*. Edited by Saʿīd al-Qazqī. Beirut: Dār al-Gharb al-Islāmī, 1992.

Mālik b. Anas. *al-Muwaṭṭaʾ*. Edited by Muḥammad Fuʾād ʿAbd al-Bāqī. Cairo: Dār Iḥyāʾ al-Kutub al-ʿArabiyya, n.d.

Muslim b. al-Ḥajjāj al-Qushayrī al-Nīsābūrī. *al-Jāmiʿ al-ṣaḥīḥ* = *Ṣaḥīḥ Muslim*. Edited by Muḥammad Fuʾād ʿAbd al-Bāqī. Cairo and Beirut: Dār Iḥyāʾ al-Kutub al-ʿArabiyya, 1954.

al-Nasāʾī, Aḥmad b. Shuʿayb. *Sunan al-Nasāʾī*. Cairo: al-Maṭbaʿat al-Maymaniyya, 1312/1894; repr. Beirut: Dār al-Kitāb al-ʿArabī.

al-Qurṭubī, Muḥammad b. Aḥmad. *Jāmiʿ li-aḥkām al-Qurʾān*. Edited by Aḥmad ʿAbd al-ʿAlīm al-Bardūnī. Repr. Beirut: Dār al-Iḥyāʾ al-Turāth al-ʿArabī, 1985.

al-Rāfiʿī, ʿAbd al-Karīm b. Muḥammad. *al-ʿAzīz: Sharḥ al-Wajīz al-maʿrūf bi-l-sharḥ al-kabīr*. Edited by ʿĀdil Aḥmad, ʿAbd al-Mawjūd, and ʿAlī Muḥammad Muʿawwaḍ. Beirut: Dār al-Kutub al-ʿIlmiyya, 1997.

al-Ramhurmuzī, al-Ḥasan b. ʿAbd al-Raḥmān. *al-Muḥaddith al-fāṣil bayna al-rāwī wa-l-wāʿī*. Edited by Muḥammad ʿAjjāj al-Khaṭīb. Beirut: Dār al-Fikr, 1984.

al-Shāfiʿī, Muḥammad b. Idrīs. *al-Umm*. Edited by Rifʿat Fawzī ʿAbd al-Muṭṭalib. Cairo: Dār al-Wafāʾ, 2001.

al-Suyūṭī, ʿAbd al-Raḥmān b. Abī Bakr. *al-Durr al-manthur fī l-tafsīrī bi-maʾthur*. Beirut: Dār al-Fikr, 2002.

al-Ṭabarānī, Sulaymān b. Aḥmad. *al-Duʿāʾ*. Edited by Muḥammad Saʿīd al-Bukhārī. Riyadh: Maktabat al-Rushd, 2008.

al-Ṭabarānī, Sulaymān b. Aḥmad. *al-Muʿjam al-awsaṭ*. Edited by Maḥmūd al-Ṭaḥḥān. Riyadh[?]: Maktabat al-Maʿārif, 1985.

al-Ṭabarānī, Sulaymān b. Aḥmad. *al-Muʿjam al-kabīr*. Edited by Ḥamdī ʿAbd al-Majīd al-Salafī. Beirut: Dār Iḥyāʾ al-Turāth al-ʿArabī, n.d.

al-Ṭabarī, Muḥammad b. Jarīr. *Tafsīr al-Ṭabarī = Jāmiʿ al-bayān*. Beirut and Amman: Dār Ibn Ḥazm and Dār al-ʿĀlam, 2002.

al-Thaʿlabī, Aḥmad b. Muḥammad. *Tafsīr al-Thaʿlabī = al-Kashf wa-l-bayyān*. Edited by Abū Muḥammad b. ʿĀshūr. Beirut: Dār Iḥyāʾ al-Turāth al-ʿArabī, 2002.

al-Tirmidhī, Muḥammad b. ʿĪsā. *Sunan al-Tirmidhī = al-Jāmiʿ al-ṣaḥīḥ*. Edited by Aḥmad Shākir, Muḥammad Fuʾād ʿAbd al-Bāqī, and Ibrāhīm ʿAṭwa. Beirut: Dār Iḥyāʾ al-Turāth al-ʿArabī, n.d. [repr. Cairo, 1938 edition].

al-Zabīdī, Muḥammad Murtaḍā, *Itḥāf al-sadā al-muttaqīn bi-sharḥ Iḥyāʾ ʿulūm al-dīn*. [Cairo]: al-Maṭbaʿ al-Maymūniyya, 1311/1894.

Index of Qurʾānic Verses

Index of *Ḥadīth*

God سُبْحَانَهُ, will bring three people into heaven for a single pilgrimage, 84
… God تَعَالَىٰ has appointed for his tomb an angel who conveys to him the salutations of anyone of his community who greets him, 110
God has replaced them for us with combat for His cause and the repetition of the *takbīr* at every rise, 94
God is greater! [I do this] in obedience to the All-Merciful, 66
God تَعَالَىٰ looks on the people of the earth each night, 12
God promised that every year six hundred thousand will make pilgrimages, 10
God تَعَالَىٰ said, 'If I wished to destroy the world, 13
God will raise up a certain people to me who will say, "O Muḥammad! O Muḥammad!," 108

ḥadīth of Gabriel: And tell me (O Muḥammad), what is Islam, 20 n.76
Here I am at Your service, O God, 37
Here I am at Your service and for Your pleasure, 37
Here I am at Your service on a pilgrimage in truth, in complete devotion and submission, 96
He who blesses me once God blesses tenfold, 110
He who imitates a folk becomes one of them, 104

I am the first on whom the earth will split open [on the day of resurrection], 11
I commit to God's safekeeping your *dīn*, 29
I enjoin on you journeying by night, 32–33
If someone comes to me as a visitor, 74
Increase circumambulations (*ṭawāf*) of this house before it is raised up, 13
Increase [your] circumambulations of the house, 6
In the name of God, God is greater. O God, from You, in You, and to You, 66
I see this color red is predominant, 90
I used to forbid you from visiting tombs, 17

Learn your rites from me, 88

Making the visit (*ʿumra*) in Ramaḍān is like performing the pilgrimage with me, 11
May you remain in God's protection and shelter, 29
The most grievous sin is for someone to be present at ʿArafa and think that God تَعَالَىٰ will not forgive him, 106
The most sinful of people is someone who stands at ʿArafa and thinks that God تَعَالَىٰ will not forgive him, 6

No one endures the hardships and severity of Medina except that I will be his intercessor on the day of resurrection, 16

When the end of time draws near, people will go on the pilgrimage in four [different groups], 83
Whoever completes seven circuits of the house [Kaʿba]…, 49
Whoever dies and has not made the pilgrimage—he should die as either a Jew or a Christian, whichever he wants, 2
Whoever finds his provision in something, he should stay with it, 18
Whoever finds wealth and does not come to me has neglected me, 74
Whoever leaves his house, goes to the mosque of Qubāʾ, 80
Whoever performs the pilgrimage to the house and avoids any obscenity or lewdness, 4

You are the best place on God's earth!, 16

Index of Supplications and Invocations

Index of People and Places

Subject Index

About the Translator

Michael Abdurrahman Fitzgerald

Originally from California, Abdurrahman Fitzgerald and his wife migrated to Morocco in the late 1970s. Since that time, he has been involved in education and the study of Arabic, Islam, and Sufism. He co-translated *Ibn al-Qayyim on the Invocation of God* (Islamic Texts Society, 2000), edited and annotated Denys Johnson-Davies's translation of al-Ghāzali's *Kitāb ādab al-akl* (Islamic Texts Society, 2000), and assisted in Kenneth Honerkamp's edition of *al-Rasāʾil al-kubrā* by Ibn ʿAbbād (Dār al-Machreq, 2005). He translated al-Ghazālī's *The Mysteries of the Prayer* (book 4), *The Mysteries of Charity* (book 5), *The Mysteries of Fasting* (book 6) of the *Revival of the Religious Sciences* (Fons Vitae), as well as the present work. Other works he has translated with Fouad Aresmouk include *The Immense Ocean*, a portion of Ibn ʿAjība's Qurʾānic commentary; *The Book of Ascension*, Ibn ʿAjība's spiritual glossary; *Two Sufi Commentaries*; and *The Mysteries of Purification*, book 3 of the *Revival of the Religious Sciences*, all published by Fons Vitae. Abdurrahman holds degrees from the University of California and Shenandoah University, Virginia, and is the director of the Center for Language and Culture, Marrakesh.